"So What?"

TEACHING CHILDREN WHAT MATTERS IN MATH

Tim Brandy

HEINEMANN
Portsmouth, NH

To Karen Dalrymple and Pat Scalo

Thanks to Sue De Marinis Brandy and Katie Brandy

Heinemann
A division of Reed Elsevier Inc.
361 Hanover Street
Portsmouth, NH 03801–3912
www.heinemann.com

Offices and agents throughout the world

© 1999 by Tim Brandy

All rights reserved. No part of this book may be reproduced in any form or by any electronic or mechanical means, including information storage and retrieval systems, without permission in writing from the publisher, except by a reviewer, who may quote brief passages in a review.

The author and publisher thank those who generously gave permission to reprint borrowed material:

Sample problem on page 46 from Oregon Questions 5 (Fall 1997), Oregon Department of Education. Reprinted by permission.

Library of Congress Cataloging-in-Publication Data
Brandy, Tim.
    So what? : teaching children what matters in math / Tim Brandy.
      p. cm.
    Includes bibliographical references.
    ISBN 0-325-00176-6
    1. Mathematics—Study and teaching (Elementary). I. Title. II. Title: Teaching children what matters in math
    QA135.5 .B6785 1999
    372.7—dc21
                                                                                               99-35787
                                                                                                           CIP

Consulting Editor: Susan Ohanian
Production: Melissa L. Inglis
Cover design: Jenny Jensen Greenleaf
Cover illustration: Kate Brandy
Manufacturing: Louise Richardson

Printed in the United States of America on acid-free paper
Docutech T & C 2007

Contents

FOREWORD *by Susan Ohanian*   v

INTRODUCTION   vii

1   The Disintegration of Math   1

2   Mathematics as an Extension of Culture   17

3   Watch Your Language   32

4   The Continuous Learning Community   56

5   Unpolluting Ourselves, Unpolluting Others   64

6   Don't Hold That Pencil, It Takes Half as Long   74

7   Talking It Out   85

8   Of Algorithms, Algebra, and Content   97

9   When Complexity Catches Up   111

10   So What?   118

Foreword

Tim Brandy's classroom is a good place for children to be. And it's a good place for teacher colleagues to visit in the pages of this book. Tim invites us into the world of a thoughtful teacher, showing us that as he tries to foster his students' mathematical understanding, he stands not on a stack of standardized test scores but on the shoulders of Piaget, Krishnamurti, Rudolph Steiner, Vivian Paley, Herb Kohl, Karen Dalrymple, his district curriculum director and mentor, *Ramona, Age 8*, Michael Crichton, and C. S. Lewis, as well as Pythagoras, al-Kworismi, Descartes, Newton, and Edward Lorenz. These are some of the giants who inform Tim's work with Sonja, Claire, Luke, Rick, and Marco—and the countless other children whose mathematical thinking we explore in these pages.

Tim invites us inside his classroom to "listen in" as he takes his instructional cues not from the cultural imperatives of media headlines but from the specific, individual needs of the children in his care. This is a teacher who cares a lot about language. Combining erudition and humor, Tim invites us to think about the language of algorithms, the language of the playground, and the needs of children.

Tim is quick to point out that this is not a "how to" book of activities but rather a book of classroom possibilities. Tim invites the reader to accompany him on his journey with children as together they explore big ideas in mathematics and create a classroom culture. It is important to realize that the mathematics of this classroom is deeply embedded in the culture: You can't have one without the other. Children learn multiplication not out of set of textbook rituals but in what Tim refers to as a *continuous learning community*, a community that includes Tim's best hopes and plans as well as the child's uncle who offers instruction in a ritualized short cut that seems to sabotage Tim's constructivist ideals. Tim's wonderful account of what he and the children learn from "the lurking poison method" is what teaching is all about.

"So What?" is filled with pedagogical insights, tips, and ongoing questions. Tim is not a teacher who makes inflated claims. He does not declare himself a master of his universe but rather states quietly "I think I am making progress." He hopes the story of his ongoing journey of becoming a teacher who follows the lead of children will encourage other teachers as well as help them to see they are not alone on their own journeys.

—Susan Ohanian

Introduction

Pablo Casals is one of the greatest cellists of all time. At the age of ninety-five, he was interviewed by a reporter who asked him why he still practiced the cello for six hours every day. His reply was "I think I'm making progress." Teaching, like cello playing, requires practice. We work daily with children responding, revising, and reflecting. Imperceptibly at first, our responses begin to match the situation. We find that we can address the learner in the moment of learning. We develop the subtle skills that transform teaching to an art.

After observing me work with a child in math, a student teacher asked me, "How did you know what to say?" I began to reflect. I knew because I knew the child. I recognized the process she was attempting to apply. I knew of other children who had been stuck in a similar place and how they had worked their way out of it. Children can construct elaborate and sophisticated math strategies. Twenty years of listening, watching, and reflecting has enabled me to construct my philosophy of teaching.

When faced with the prospect of writing a math book, I was excited. It wasn't that I considered myself to be a master of mathematics or education. Rather, it was that I believed I had been making progress in recent years. With an interest in writing, I looked forward to the challenge of articulating my experiences, reflections, and thoughts about teaching math. I wanted to share the change I noticed in children's thinking and work as they approached math from their own perspective. Believing there were other practicing and prospective teachers who were considering similar classroom strategies, I decided to write a book that could serve both as an affirmation and a prompt for them.

Children are natural learners. It is part of the definition of childhood. Learning naturally includes math. Math is one way they make sense of and communicate about the world. In my work with children, I have witnessed the derivation of the associative law of multiplication and the discovery of aliquots, algebraic sums, and countless theorems, axioms, conditions, and identities. I have seen eight-, nine-, and ten-year-olds recreate the foundation of algebra, geometry, and calculus. This is logical since the same human brain that created the entire framework for the field of mathematics exists within the child. The child is capable of discovering everything we know in math.

When we attempt to impose the historically constructed mathematical framework onto children, it is unauthentic, even coercive. It is foreign to their sense. They ask, "So what?" and "What does it matter?" Rather than being sarcastic or confrontational, this question offers us the opportunity to delve into our own understanding and beliefs about teaching. The four-year-old learns because it matters. The continuum of learning will remain intact as long as we don't interfere. It is our responsibility to find what matters for children and create the environment where the possibility of pursuit exists.

This is not a "how to" book. There are no activities to apply to your classroom. I won't say how or what a teacher should teach to a group of children I have never met. Such a task would be preposterous and I a fool for trying. Rather, this book is about my philosophy and values as a teacher. I share the experiences and thought processes that have led me to my present approach. It is a reflection. I share it so you won't feel alone in your questions and follies. I hope that it allows you to create new thoughts and pursue new questions for yourself.

I arranged the themes of this book according to the way I organize my thoughts about teaching. After beginning with a historical and social foundation for my belief in the arbitrary nature of the traditional math curriculum, I created chapters that reflect the way I learned while working with children. Each chapter is a complete idea. It is not necessary to read them sequentially. Each is illustrated by the stories of my work with children. This is followed by my reflection about an experience and embedded in my pedagogy. Children offered their thinking and their stories to me as an opportunity for me to understand the relationship between teacher, child, and context. In the same way, I offer this book as my story of becoming a teacher who follows the lead of children. This is the story of how I answered "so what?" for myself as a teacher. It is an opportunity for you to wonder and reflect about teaching. It exists because I think I am making progress.

1
The Disintegration of Math

> *Once upon a time people solved systems of linear equations by elimination. Then somebody invented determinants and Cramer's rule and everybody learned that. Now determinants are regarded as old-fashioned and cumbersome, and it is considered better to solve systems of linear equations by elimination.*
>
> —R. P. BOAS, JR.
> 1958

In the first grade, one-to-one correspondence and counting are taught. By the end of the year, children will be able to count to one hundred. Simple addition will be easily computed. Second graders learn to add larger numbers that involve regrouping. They subtract simple terms. They are introduced to borrowing. Third grade is the year of operations. Children become proficient at regrouping in subtraction, learn multiplication facts and computation, and are introduced to division....

So goes the scope and sequence of math. Slight variations and fluctuations occur, but the same general idea is found in textbooks published from 1930 through 1998. The addition of color, charts, and graphs, motivational slogans, designer clothes, and idiomatic language does not mask the similarity in mathematical content. Our math education is grounded in twentieth-century culture, but has math always been ordered this way? Do we stop and consider why this sequence is taught? Do we know its origins? Can we imagine different ways to approach math curriculum?

The Well-Oiled Machine and the Disintegration of Math Curriculum

Isaac Newton is known as the "father of modern science." His investigations of force have guided technology, science, and mathematics into the twentieth century. Newton observed events, then worked out mathematical formulas to demonstrate and explain them. Developing mathematical principles, he published them in a famous and influential book called *Principia Mathematica*. Another mathematician and scientist, René Descartes, attempted to capture, in diagram and formula, the workings of the planets. His theories ended up establishing the fields of algebra and geometry. For these and other mathematicians of the seventeenth century, mathematics was a tool to organize, communicate, and convince others of their hypotheses. The establishment of math as an independent study was not their intention.

Following the work of Newton, Descartes, and other mathematicians of their time, the fields of science and technology expanded. The way was paved for the industrial revolution. Simple principles were repeated and iterated into complex ideas. In the two centuries after their publications, the field of mathematics emerged as individuals dedicated their work to the refinement and reformulation of these principles and strategies. The goal was to make mathematics neat and logical—a well-oiled machine. Uniformity was the order of the day.

In developing sequence and scope, mathematicians pushed thinking into separate categories. One person focused on geometry while another worked with algebra. Computations became so complex that the study of equations began to emerge as an independent pursuit. Specific language resulted. By the end of the nineteenth century, compartmentalization and reductionism in mathematics was accepted. Complex problems were reduced to elemental principles and specific skills.

During this time, mathematics education was treated as a science. Formulas were esteemed because they led to reproducible solutions. Mathematics education began to resemble its industrial counterpart—the assembly line. Rules were established for the efficient calculation of problems. Certain sequences of instruction became normative. The hierarchy for teaching was forged. Experts determined where, when, and what mathematical skills and concepts would be taught. A sequence of concepts was prescribed for elementary school. Prerequisites to high-school and college classes were developed. The art of investigative math was replaced with an established scope and sequence. In the new course of math, one would accumulate skills in prescribed order.

Continued segregation of operations led to a serious disintegration of mathematics. The practice of developing skills by involving all available mathematic operations, geometry, and algebra during inquiry was reduced. Students' ability to simultaneously utilize operations was restricted. Instead, one operation at a time was introduced and mastered. The interrelationship of operations was not considered important.

Mathematical Disenfranchisement

The farmer at the turn of the century still knew how to estimate the number of bales of hay that would fit in the barn and how much feed livestock needed for winter. Train engineers continued to calculate times of arrival with notable precision. Orchardists still knew how many crates to amass for harvest. Currency exchange replaced barter in the culture. Houses were planned, lumber purchased, and buildings completed.

But the math of school began to diverge from the cultural math. Scope and sequence ignored daily cultural practice. Instead, it reflected the historical development of mathematical concepts in continental history. Students would learn mathematic principles according to the order these had evolved historically. Rooted in complex formulas, instruction was reduced to simplistic terms. Once reduced, mathematics educators mapped the given path from the simple to the complex, forming a dogmatic system of teaching. Sometimes the order was not apparent to the creators of scope and sequence. This was the case in geometry and algebra. Their order was decided on the basis of the alphabet, hence *algebra* precedes *geometry*. It is important to note that mathematical sequence was determined by a particular group of math educators. It was established out of a best-guess process.

This new "science" of math was pure. Mathematic investigators of the early century focused on such endeavors as finding the tenth perfect number, prime numbers, square roots, and odd numbers. They were exploring math simply for the extension of the concepts. The study was an end in itself. A schism occurred in the culture between math and the "real" world.

Math of the culture did not diminish, but was slowly discredited. Estimation was expelled from the classroom. With the power no longer in their hands, people began to perceive their everyday math work differently. In fact, it was not even considered math. Similar patterns emerged in other school subjects. Science was no longer the art of a curious individual honing observation skills, recording, and creating generalizations. Astronomy became the art of learning names other cultures had assigned to the stars, devoid of the mystery and meaning a current culture might create. Spelling was standardized. Even libraries were organized around one person's idea of a convenient way to locate books.

Elementary school became the assembly line for algorithmic math. Children were taught to memorize formulas burned into their brains through repeated practice. The language of teaching math became standard. Words borrowed from the culture, such as product and multiple, became institutionalized as mathematical language in the schools, their cultural meaning atrophied.

Students whose thinking patterns diverged from standard sequences failed. It was not a consequence of competency, discipline, or application, but a question of match. If one's pattern of learning matched the pattern assumed by the standard practices, success followed. If not, failure was probable. Today, we continue to be rooted in one hundred fifty years of dogma, learning the sequence of thinking of people who came before us.

Personal Disintegration and the Reintegration of Math for the Child

Anna was a fifth grader who had entered my class at the beginning of her fourth grade year. Her previous school had a class size of six, so with the twenty-six children in this new class, she was initially shy. She would approach me after minilessons and directions and ask me to repeat and re-explain the directions. After three weeks, I began to ask *her* to repeat the directions. She could do so without hesitation and only wanted to be assured that she had understood correctly. Beginning her work, she wanted to check with me to see if she was proceeding "right." Again, I waited a couple of weeks, then asked if she thought she was heading in the right direction. During math workshop she was unsure of herself, didn't risk experimentation and was relatively unproductive. All of this behavior surprised me because I found her to be articulate with language and adept in algorithm procedures.

Realizing that we would spend two years together allowed me to revise my short- and long-term expectations for her. In a conference, I described my observations and confusion to her. When she responded that she felt confused and unsure, I asked her to allow me to direct her work in a review of math processes and number concepts. I believed that our mathematical foundations were different. Anna had been taught algorithms devoid of meaning. Her thinking and work was based on a teacher's set of rules. This person was the "gatekeeper" of mathematical knowledge. Success depended on remembering and following the rules to a correct solution. Suddenly, I was asking her to extend her work based on understanding of previously learned concepts. I wanted her to behave as a mathematical pioneer the same way that Isaac Newton and René Descartes had behaved. The ability to solve problems lies in the capacity to find a place within a student's own mathematical infrastructure from which to proceed. Faced with unfamiliar problems, a child needs to select a starting point rooted in understanding and proceed using logical thinking to a solution that makes sense.

Anna was willing to revisit these fundamental concepts of numeracy and quickly built her understanding of concepts. She could use language and logic to reduce problems into workable parts, then articulate her reasoning. Her anxiety was replaced by a yearning to know. She didn't forget her formulas. Instead, Anna took pride in knowing many ways to solve problems. The excitement of learning things by herself motivated her. Instead of a gatekeeper, Anna viewed me as a resource.

But in Math It's Different

Laura wanted to try to solve equations involving the multiplication of a mixed number and a whole number. Here was her first problem.

$$\begin{array}{r} 86 \\ \times\ 12\frac{1}{2} \\ \hline \end{array}$$

Laura's understanding of fractions came from time spent drawing and cutting whole shapes into equally sized parts. She had used fraction blocks to learn equivalent sizes. Set diagrams and graphs were part of her personal "tool kit" for solving problems. She had figured out that one half times a number could be translated into one half of the number. Her problem progressed as she wrote:

$$\begin{array}{r} 86 \\ \times\ 12\frac{1}{2} \\ \hline 1723 \\ +\ 86 \\ \hline 1809 \end{array}$$

She came to me with her work because she wasn't sure how to check her answer and she didn't think it was right. I asked Laura to explain her work.

"Well, I know that one half times six is three. So I wrote that down. Then I started with the two. Oops. I forgot one half times eight. Don't I need to do that?"

I told her that this made sense to me. Laura pulled out her eraser and changed the problem.

$$\begin{array}{r} 86 \\ \times\ 12\frac{1}{2} \\ \hline 17243 \\ +\ 86 \\ \hline 17329 \end{array}$$

"Wow! That's a big number. I think I'm doing something wrong."

I was pleased that Laura realized that the answer didn't seem correct but I saw her procedure as a breakdown in mathematical thinking. She was trying to take too many new steps and had lost her connection to the understanding of the whole problem. I tried to get her to take a step back. Using the language of place value I asked her to read the multiplicand. After her response of eighty-six, I attempted to break the problem into parts using her language of place value.

"One half times eight equals four, but does this number really have eight ones?"

"No, it's eight tens. Eighty."

"What is one half times eighty?"

"Well it means one half of eighty. In real, one half of eighty equals forty ones or four tens, but in math it's different. Four tens doesn't always go in the tens place."

Where had Laura lost the connection? How had math disintegrated within her? Why wouldn't four tens go into the tens place? What did she mean by "real"? Somehow, she had learned not to trust her math thinking. Real could be separate from math.

At times like this I can easily feel dismay. I assume that children understand concepts. Instead, they have lost touch with the foundation of their knowledge. Mathematical integration has been lost. Realizing this, I check myself before proceeding. I don't want to continue when I am feeling upset with my practices because children sense my frustration and it is the frustration that they take away from the lesson. The intensity of the emotion is a more forceful teacher than the content of the lesson. I also don't proceed when I sense that the children feel they have failed. Directing work through periods of strong feelings usually results in failure. If the strong feelings are mine, I might become invested in reaching a "successful conclusion" that is a correct answer. This is at the expense of building the language, logic, and confidence that problem solving requires. It leaves the children stranded. If the strong feelings belong to the children, the work we do will be secondary and won't have a long-term benefit. Instead, at these times, I ask the children to table this work and redirect them to other tasks until later. I tell them that I want to think about the problem and work through it sensibly. I keep a notebook in which I write anecdotal information on each child. Twice a month, I choose a specific skill and systematically note each child's proficiency with that skill. In between these observations, I record observations of their work, problems they have or breakthroughs they make. In preparation to work with a child, I refer to my notes to find a starting place where their knowledge and process is solid.

In Laura's case, I was more curious than dismayed. My first thought was that Laura meant "real" the way teachers talk about real—applied work outside of the classroom. I asked Laura what she meant by "real."

"You know, like if I had eighty beads and I wanted to save half of them, that would be forty. But in problems like this, forty doesn't fit."

There were two things I wanted out of this work with Laura. I wanted her to reintegrate math and "real" and I wanted her to develop a strategy that could direct her to a solution. Merging a child's knowledge of the world with abstract problems requires finding a point where the connection is grounded and obvious to the child. Children participate mathematically during their interpretation and communication of daily life. Sometimes it is as basic as counting and drawing. It might be in their language of "more than" and "less than" or even in "mine" and "yours." It means stepping away from the immediate problem and refocusing from a larger picture. This is always the starting point of reintegration.

I wanted her to see the multiplication of a mixed number and whole number as simply a matter of building the problem from sensible parts.

$$86 \times 12\tfrac{1}{2}$$

If she considers eighty-six to be a set, the twelve and one half occurrences of this set can be extrapolated. Working with her example of beads, I began to ask her to visualize the repetitive sets.

"Laura, think of collecting a large group of beads. You want to find out how many you have altogether. Suppose you put them in piles of eighty-six because it takes eighty-six beads to make a necklace. You have twelve and a half groups. You want to find out how many beads you have. How can you find out?"

Laura thought for a minute. "That's easy. I know that ten groups will equal eight hundred and sixty. Then I can add two more groups. Then one half of a group."

Laura recorded these figures in her math log and completed a sequence of adding. When she was finished she had an answer. To bring her work into agreement with the algorithmic form she was used to, we simply reorganized her numbers. We recorded in two different ways so that she could see that the work could have different forms, each reflecting different subprocesses. We could use either way as long as the relationship of the process to the problem was evident.

86		86	
x 12½		x 12½	
43	(½ x 86)	172	(2 x 86)
172	(2 x 86)	+ 860	(10 x 86)
+ 860	(10 x 86)	1032	(12 x 86)
1075	(12½ x 86)	+ 43	(½ x 86)
		1075	(12½ x 86)

Laura had initiated this conversation and work with me out of curiosity. Having selected a direction in math workshop, she was motivated. My task was to help her derive a method that made sense without discouragement.

Those Who Can and Those Who Can't

I have two adults who regularly work in math workshop. Linda is a special education teacher who spends time assisting children who are on an individualized education plan because they have been designated as having learning problems. Each week, she spends two hours in class. When there, she works with all students. Linda loved math in school. She was quite successful, received "good grades," and progressed through geometry, algebra, and trigonometry in high school. In college, she completed statistics and calculus.

When Linda comes into our math workshop she feels intimidated. She understands and believes in the philosophy that children should construct their own strategies and concepts. She believes that the independent derivation of processes empowers children. However, she had been given the processes as rules and steps in calculation. Because she learned these rules easily, she never had to consider the reasons for them. Even as a very competent calculator, she still has trouble constructing steps leading to algorithms. Process articulation is foreign. With all of her mathematical training, the questions asked by children make her uncomfortable. As an adult teacher, she expects to know strategies and her natural tendency is to show them to children. It is difficult for her to watch students calculating problems with methods she considers cumbersome. When the class works with problems that have many solutions or take logical analysis, Linda is unsure of her teaching role. Always, she is amazed at the level of thinking and work of the children. She laments that she was never taught why the rules work. Knowing that following rules led her to the "right" answer satisfied her until she began to work with children to develop their own thinking. For the first time she was faced with the disintegration of her own mathematical thinking.

Through conversations, Linda and I decided that everyone would be better served if she took some time to become a student in the class. Shedding the role of teacher freed her to experiment with problems, strategies, and materials. In doing this, she was able to shore up her algorithms with meaningfully constructed concepts. At the same time, her work served as a role model for the children.

Jackie is a teacher and music specialist. She never felt successful in math during her school years. Rules and concepts floated around in her early learning and didn't ground themselves into reasonable order so that she could remember and use them. In music, order produced a song. In math, the product was dissonant. Jackie is an avid sports person, riding bikes for thousands of miles, backpacking, skiing, and more. Her ability to plan and estimate in life is outstanding. In music, she can transpose keys fluently. She ended up in our math workshop because she had extra time. She felt uncomfortable because math reminded her of her own unsuccessful classroom experiences. I noticed Jackie, like Linda, looking for a solution, then showing children the prescribed pathway to it.

With time, Jackie grew to value the workshop because she was able to make sense out of the problems by working with the children. It wasn't long before she began to think of the math in the things she does in her everyday life and recreation. At the same time, she developed comfort in math work with children.

Linda and Jackie represent the disintegration of cultural math and pure math. Linda is an expert in pure math, a dancer of formulas and solutions. Jackie is a master of cultural math, an artist of estimation and application. Yet neither of them feel whole in their math. As educators learn to reintegrate math in their classrooms, they will become versed in both aspects of math. It is then that they will empower children to accurately use mathematical calculation in everyday life while using the reasoning of everyday life in math class.

Mathematics: Who Needs It?

There is a poster in the high school math classroom that depicts mathematical training and its use as a hierarchy, correlating it to careers. On the lowest step of math application is the career of housewife. According to the poster, a housewife needs only the basic operations of addition, subtraction, multiplication, and division. The highest step in this corollary is the physicist. This career will require all the concepts one will learn in algebra, trigonometry, and calculus. In between, many careers are listed according to their mathematical sophistication. Teachers rank below computer programmers but above bank tellers.

This poster is a visual reference point in the classroom. Children notice it and talk about it positively. It is concise and absolute, appealing to students on many levels. Some reflect on the career prestige that it represents. Intelligence correlates to math complexity and prestige. But the poster is misleading. It depicts a sexist attitude in gender-specific career names such as "housewife." Less apparent are the fundamental assumptions. What is the author referring to as math? The hierarchy derived suggests answer-driven pencil and paper skills. In the case of the "housewife" we are supposed to imagine the use of basic operations in balancing checkbooks, budgeting, generating quantities for shopping lists, and calculating ingredients for recipes. But what about the myriad of other exercises all of us undertake in daily activities? There is geometry in driving through town, statistics in choosing a quick route to the bank and algebra in deciding how many pancakes to make for breakfast. Estimation and missing variables infuse our daily life. This occurs so routinely that we no longer view them as mathematical strategies. But they are.

A few years ago, a middle school teacher came to me and asked that I not use the word *algebra* in my math class. I couldn't really be teaching "algebra." He thought that my premature use of this term took the mystique away from his seventh-grade class. I believe this very mystique causes a separation in children between their everyday mathematical experience and classroom work. It is this mystique that builds and reinforces the notion that there is not a connection between "real" and math. Rather, it is our responsibility to reintroduce the terminology back into the cultural context from which it derived.

Any missing addend or product represents a variable and therefore leads us into algebra. If I ask, "What is the answer to four plus three?" I am asking a child to calculate the equation $4 + 3 = n$ where n can stand for any number. It is algebra just as counting is a numerical sequence pattern with an interval of one. Multiplication patterns simply require changing this interval to another number. By allowing children to know the language and concepts of math whenever they occur for them, we strengthen their belief that math is integrated naturally. Complex formulas and ideas are rooted in simple concepts and equations.

I Can't Make Change

My daughter Katie's third grade report card clearly demonstrated that she could add, subtract, multiply, and divide numbers with varying degrees of difficulty. It stated that she knew her addition, subtraction, and multiplication facts fluently. I know it well because I wrote it. I was her teacher. She continued her math education through high-school algebra receiving letter grade equivalents of average or above. She scored within the average range on college entrance exams. In preparation for college, she opened a checking account. Knowing she had successfully-completed a class in family living, I assumed she knew how to maintain her balance in a check register. Being a protective father, I asked her to review this with me before leaving for college. We looked at the register and I talked about tracking checks, subtracting the amount from the previous balance, and determining how much money she currently had in her account. She looked at me sheepishly and said that she'd try to keep it up but that she really couldn't subtract. That third grade year flashed into my mind. I recalled her success with algorithms. I couldn't understand and asked her to clarify. She said that the only way she subtracted was with a calculator.

What had happened to Katie in the nine years since her third grade experience? Had her ability atrophied from dependence on a calculator and lack of mental use? Had she ever understood subtraction or *any* of the math she had encountered? According to Katie, a series of steps led to this demise in math. In middle school, she had been ashamed to be smart. Certain girls had made fun of her, so she quit asking questions and took on a less assertive role in her education. It was easier to be silent with the hope that she could figure out assignments on her own. Her goal was to complete the work. Copying assignments and retaining sufficient knowledge of formulas to pass a test was all that mattered.

Later, a series of teachers had confused her with formulas and procedures she didn't understand. Asking for explanation was not the norm in the classroom environment. When she did ask, she felt silly and misunderstood. Teachers simply repeated the information without trying to understand her confusion. There was never time to understand one concept before moving on to the next. The priority was to demonstrate proficiency and move on. Dialogue was nonexistent. In fact, no one was talking except the teacher. Children would caucus before and after class to share homework and check answers. What built up in place of math understanding was an intricate network of deception that allowed Katie to score adequately on tests and pass classes. She was masking a self-image of math inadequacy.

I spent a lot of time reflecting on this failure of our educational system for such an intelligent child. It was easy to blame other teachers. I had entrusted them with a competent, confident child. But I knew that I had been part of the system. My math curriculum of eleven years ago had been driven by solutions to problems rather than concept construction and understanding.

Katie assumed an attitude of math failure and lack of confidence. Determined to rectify the situation, I brought home my manipulatives assuring Katie that I could supply her with processes and understandings easily. We worked, but her frustration intensified. Unsuccessfully, I tried to find the point of her misunderstanding. Finally, we decided to set aside this work. She would tell me when and how I might help.

During the summer following her freshman year, she got a job at a coffee shop. A great fear was actualized when she had to learn to make and count back change. Fighting her apprehension of exposure as a math failure, she began. She took it slowly and carefully at first, gaining confidence with each transaction. Within a few weeks, she wasn't even aware of the effort it took to make these transactions. Having freed herself from classroom math, she began to rebuild math concepts and practices. The difference was that she chose the skills and derived the process for her thinking. The rift of disintegration began to close in Katie's math thinking.

Most children grow up mathematically. It is part of their everyday culture. Through reflecting on Katie and the math stories of many children, I came to understand the damage I can cause in children's thinking when I "give" them math concepts that sometimes differ from and disregard their self-derived math knowledge. It causes a separation in their belief about math. This separation is their personal disintegration of math.

Math News and Societal Disintegration

Today in the news, an earthquake measuring 5.3 on the Richter scale rocked the coast of Chile. Economists expected the Leading Economic Index to be up. The Gross National Product held steady this year. Reports indicate that the results of the National Assessment will be available within a few weeks. Medicare costs have risen 12 percent over the last eighteen months. The ozone depletion continues with the hole over the Antarctic now 25 percent greater than last year. The United States Forest Service presented a rebuttal to the report given by the Sierra Club about millions of dollars lost in the process of timber sales on federal land. The news is full of math. In fact, it is so full of math that most listeners don't understand the figures, much less their derivation. Clear statements of rationale and data collection are rare. Readers are not given the formula used to obtain the statistic. Yet the data remains powerful, unequivocable.

We assume numbers are constant. They are among the last "facts" in a society where science is questioned and revised while values emerge and fluctuate. Mathematical statistics are given supreme status. Math in the news constitutes "pure" information. When politicians use numbers, few argue. This can become an inexpensive "slight of hand" with potential to direct public thinking. True meaning and intention can be veiled because the listeners are separated from the mathematical foundations that create the statistics. We find the statistical processes tedious or confusing. When statistics are reported in the news, we learn more from the tone of the reporter's voice than from extrapolating and evaluating the information. The result can be an artificial sense of well-being or woe.

Is this ignorance a result of the way we teach math in school? Has education participated in this disintegration of math between the reporter and listener? In classrooms, we often teach children that we are the "gatekeeper" of math knowledge as a by-product of our environment, expectations, and activities. As teachers we dole formulas out at appropriate times and according to a scope and sequence or syllabus. These formulas prescribe the way to solutions. They are rarely constructed by students. Only those few who follow the maze of math classes into college are taught the subtle derivations for the type of the math that is used in the news.

The solution to this dilemma might include changing the reporting into information bytes that the public can understand. This, however, takes away a great deal of power from reporting agencies who are interested in controlling our opinions. Power is difficult to relinquish. A society that lacks confidence in the face of statistics will not develop the ability to demand comprehensible and responsible reporting. If we begin to teach children how to derive and evaluate statistics, tables, scales, and other measurements, they will learn to interpret the measuring devices in the news. They will choose to ignore misleading graphs and charts and utilize accurate ones to inform their thinking.

Statistical analysis is a natural part of growing up. Children know that most of their fellow students eat sugar. They also know how many abstain from sugar for health reasons. When it is time for a Valentine's party, they know how much food needs to be provided for both. They also know the ratio of boys to girls or fourth to fifth graders in class. They have rating scales for inviting friends to a birthday party or participating in a classroom work group. They predict which teams will win in a game in physical education. All of this occurs naturally without our intervention. It is possible to find ways to extend their skills into organizing, recording, and reporting information. If we can bring their natural data collection, interpretation, and analysis into math class, we will transform their practice into an important tool. Then we can teach them to utilize the newspaper as a primary source of interpreting, understanding, and assessing statistical information. Our responsibility as teachers is to understand the importance of this math strand and incorporate it into the classrooms of children who need these skills. Then, they can become competent citizens with the ability to apply this work to important decisions.

Allowing the Question to Drive the Math

Albert Einstein became known as a visionary scientist in the early 1900s. He was able to synthesize information and concepts, then make major leaps in their application to physics. Driven by new insights, he developed mathematical equations to describe his ideas and relationships. This work depended on the math and science of such predecessors as Christian Doppler, Joseph von Fraunhofer, and Edward Hubble. His advances were driven by his quest to understand and explain. His questions led him to new principles and formula development.

Similarly, Georges Lemaître's work led him to question part of Einstein's idea. Following Einstein's logic, Lemaître began to wonder about Einstein's conception of the universe as infinite and unchanging. Questioning this, he turned to mathematical equations. As his work developed, he became more and more convinced that Einstein had made a mistake. Lemaître spoke of Einstein's mistake to groups of astrophysicists, but was ignored in the wake of the latter's popularity. He persisted, driven by his own insight and bolstered by his confidence in the mathematical work he had produced. Finally, he was able to meet Einstein and share his work. At the end of their discussion, Einstein proclaimed Lemaître's argument beautiful and irrefutable. He called one particular aspect of his own theory a blunder.

Both scientists used math. Both derived new equations. Both were driven by their questions, not the math. Can we create situations with children in our classes that will allow them the excitement and satisfaction of deriving strategies and concepts as they pursue questions they choose? Can we allow them the time and support to develop their thinking? Can we stop covering textbooks and begin uncovering roadways to mathematical thinking? Can we begin a movement to reintegrate math and the world of experience in which they are involved?

The beauty of Einstein's exchange with Lemaître lies in Einstein's response. Delighting in discovery, he expressed great satisfaction even when shown his mistake. I want to behave like this in my teaching, and it starts with listening to children. Allowing the fullness of their questions and considering both their assertions and their confusion, I begin to find new ways to open pathways to assist their learning. I, too, blunder. Sometimes I don't know how to untangle a child's thinking. Sometimes I can't see a reasonable answer to their inquiries. Sometimes I forge into an explanation without due consideration. Sharing my blunders in math with parents and children demonstrates my value of the process of learning. It opens math to inquiry.

Native Plant Park: Creating a Project to Integrate

Devon's mom, Joyce, approached me one fall afternoon six years ago. She is an architect and wanted to give some time to Devon's class by bringing her skills to our curriculum. She suggested that we undertake a project which she could help direct. Through a grant, Joyce had previously worked at a high school to design a picnic area for students. We talked about our relative time commitment to a large project. We brainstormed ideas including a classroom loft and a deck on the courtyard side of the room. We decided to take the question of a project to the children.

Students were enthusiastic. They liked our ideas and added many of their own. Shannon wanted to know more about the picnic area at the high school. The discussion turned toward a project that would serve the entire school. Luke loved plants and added landscaping to the idea. Momentum grew and before I knew it, the children were discussing a park. Joyce and I exchanged looks and shrugged. This discussion occurred during a time when our region of Oregon had suffered drought for seven years. Interjecting, I asserted that any such plan would have to include water resource conservation. The children decided to explore the school park.

Their idea grew daily under our supervision and guidance. Little did I know at the time that this idea would evolve into a large-scale, long-term project that would provide a rich source of curriculum. The children focused on the lawn area in the front of the school. They worked hard to develop their ideas before presenting them to the school principal, staff, school board, and maintenance department.

During the fall and winter of that year, the project took over our math curriculum. Before presenting their ideas, the children had to determine the size of the proposed park. Driven by this need, they learned about area. Measuring desks, carpets, tile, and any flat surface in the room, they began to understand and compare areas. Then they measured the proposed park. Applying the strategies from classwork, they determined the size of the park to be forty thousand square feet. Next, they observed the proposed area over many days. They wanted to know if and how it was used. They wouldn't want to take away an important school asset. Collecting use data, they created graphs demonstrating their findings. Scale became a major part of the work. Joyce took them to her office to show how she worked with small scale models and graphs to make her designs. Working with Joyce, the children determined a workable ratio for scale. Grids were laid out in the classroom. Groups of children collaborated on design ideas. They made presentations and integrated separate ideas into a plan. After many revisions, this plan was presented by students and accepted by the staff and school board.

The work had engulfed our classroom time. I was nervous about loss of specific subject work, but I sensed the importance of the project. It was not until I heard the children make their presentations and respond to questions that I fully understood the significance of what had happened. I listened with delight as they shared their data and responded to questions. Math was evident everywhere. They talked about scale, present use, timelines, and budget proposals. This was just the beginning. One day, I was trying to figure out how many yards of mulch we would need to prepare a large area of the project. Tom asked about my work. At first, I thought it was too complicated for him. Catching myself, I explained the task. Tom became excited. He wanted to participate in this problem. Two other children joined us as we measured the area and calculated the depth to find the volume of material we needed. Tom called a lumber yard to find out the formula for converting this volume to cubic yards. As the project developed, many children learned how to figure area and order cubic yards of mill by-products and concrete. They inquired about prices for plants, compared discounts, wrote grants, and budgeted money. Math was very intentional and practical. Lessons occurred around the need to know.

Six years later, this project is still an important part of our curriculum. Children have long-term data collections about water use. They monitor plant growth. They are presently developing a partnership with a local nursery to trade plants they have propagated from seeds and cuttings for mulch and new plants. They will learn about gross and net profit, overhead, and profit margin. But most important, they know math as a tool to organize, calculate, and communicate information that they care about. Math is integrated for them.

2
Mathematics as an Extension of Culture

He was a linguist, after all and it seemed entirely possible to him that religion and literature and art and poetry and music were all simply side effects of a brain structure that comes into the world ready to make language out of noise, sense out of chaos. Our capacity for imposing meaning, he thought, is programmed to unfold the way a butterfly's wings unfold when it escapes the chrysalis, ready to fly. We are biologically driven to create meaning—and if that's so, he asked himself, is the miracle diminished?

—MARY DORIA RUSSELL
Children of God

In 1996, a small, isolated group of people lived in the jungles of South America. Their remote home had maintained physical and cultural isolation. Seldom seen, they lived peacefully hunting, gathering, and cultivating without the implements of the industrial revolution. Their land was protected as a reserve, set aside from encroachment of large agriculture and mining interests. However, a group of miners, filled with the greed that accompanies development, recognized the value of this land. Rich resources lay beneath it and the very existence of these indigenous people stood in the way of the miners' wealth. They organized an attack resulting in the massacre of all the members of the village they found. When governmental authorities learned of these atrocities, they sent military personnel to investigate. They found a few survivors but could gather little information. The practice of the villagers in the confines of this environment was to burn the bodies of the dead and consume the ashes. Like their culture, their number system was simple, present, and direct. They counted: one, two, many. Many people had died. This and their devastating sorrow constituted the entire story.

Do the Numbers Count?

The aboriginal people of Australia had no words for numbers. Yet it was important to communicate quantity and time. The large group regularly dispersed on their walkabouts into smaller groups for extended periods. When the time came for ceremonial congregation, these separate groups would appear. All of the materials for the ceremony were ready. Anthropologists had difficulty understanding these seemingly spontaneous gatherings. How did the groups, dispersed all over the vast outback, know when to gather? Instead of words, the people had developed an elaborate system of communicating time and quantity using the palm of the hand as a reference point. By pointing to specific points on the hand, they could denote given future dates or quantities.

The development of number systems grows from the need to communicate. It represents the community's requirements for successful interaction. Variables influencing number system complexity include time and space. When a culture desires posterity, the recording of its history, future planning, or a link between the mortal and eternal, more complex systems evolve. A good example of this is our present calendar. After centuries of using a lunar calendar, Rome's year became four hundred forty days long. Julius Caesar commissioned astronomer Sosigenes to develop an alternate calendar that would provide predictable and stable markings of days, dates, and events. The new calendar would allow planning and coordination of harvest and planting celebrations. Sosigenes delivered a calendar based on the solar cycle. This Julian calendar worked well for everyone except members of the Roman Catholic Church. Pope Gregory XIII wanted religious holidays based on the solstice and equinox. These events were not predictable on the Julian calendar. Hiring another astronomer, Christophe Clavious, he developed the Gregorian calendar using leap years to synchronize the solar events with religious celebrations. Today, some people see a conflict between the various religious and cultural calendars (Moslem, Chinese, Gregorian) and the interdependency of commerce and travel. Proposals have been made to form a Universal calendar.

Communication with social members far away through the media of telephone, letter, or computer network requires the language of numbers. Phone numbers are used in a complex system to designate, identify, and isolate an individual line for a specific person. When communication systems become complex, efficiency dictates a move beyond pointing and pictures. Out of the culture's needs comes the math.

In 580 B.C., Pythagoras was born on the Greek island of Samos. He lived eighty years. During this time he developed mathematical theorems which still form a basis for our thinking. In fact, his investigations into whole numbers evolved directly into the integer arithmetic we teach. Yet, all of the work of Pythagoras was done without written numbers. He studied dots in sand to derive mathematical relationships. The most considered relationship was the triangular array. A tetraktys or ten dot triangular array is depicted in the following figure.

```
            x
         x     x
      x     x     x
   x     x     x     x
```

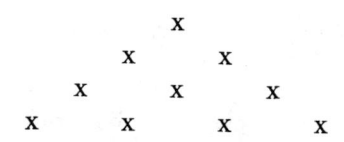

Adding the number of the points in each row of this array, we get the following equation: 1 + 2 + 3 + 4 = 10. This makes ten; a triangular number. Any number that is the sum of points in a triangular array is a triangular number. Ten is the fourth triangular number in the sequence: 1, 3, 6, 10, 15, 21. . . . These relationships have been studied extensively since 540 B.C. Centuries later, Karl Gauss determined that every whole number can be ascertained by adding three triangular numbers.

Pythagoras viewed these mathematical relationships with mystical awe. He formed secret societies, akin to the monasteries of the fifteenth century, of men and women to ponder these number relationships. Mathematical relationships were the basis of studies in science and religion. In fact, they were the foundation of the universe. They led to understanding of musical intervals, astronomical distances, laws of physics, and social constructions. Contemplation of mathematical relationships led to purification and enrichment of the soul. A student of mathematics was a student of religion.

Numbers are cultural in origin. In our present society we model counting to toddlers. We teach very young children to hold up fingers designating their age. We play games, "One for you and one for me . . ." Then as letter symbols are introduced we introduce number symbols. Children learn the importance of numbers concurrently with the practice and value of other aspects of our culture. This skill is necessary for their interaction with other members of society. Knowledge of numbers has become part of our basic literacy. In the early stages of public education, academic cornerstones were reading, writing, and arithmetic. These remain the most assessed part of children's learning today.

It helps me to remember that numbers serve a cultural function beyond themselves. For Pythagoras the purpose of number study was the purification of the soul; for us it is quantification, identification, and communication across distance and through time. Numbers allow social energy in the form of currency to cross biogeographical and political boundaries. They allow banks to hold and lend money. They are the basis of our digital lifelines from telephones to computers. They exist in correlation to our present and past need.

I was sitting at Ray's conference. As we discussed math, this third grader was demonstrating his strategies for adding numbers. The problem he considered was:

$$\begin{array}{r} 65 \\ + 47 \\ \hline \end{array}$$

He had used the tens blocks. Ray recorded his work with a symbol system for the blocks. In this system, I represented one ten. X represented a one. Ray's answer was represented like this:

<u>I I I I I I X X X X X</u>
<u>I I I X X X X X X X</u>

I I I I I I I I I I X X

As he continued to explain, Ray pointed to the two symbols. "These are tens and these are ones."

Immediately a bell went off inside of my head. I wanted to clarify. I wanted to say, "Ray, don't you mean that these (I) *stand for* tens and these (X) *stand for* ones." I wanted him to be prepared to understand relative value. I worried that the language he was using separated him from understanding the meaning of this work. At the same time, I wanted to nurture confidence in Ray as he explained this process to his parents. Fortunately, I chose the latter. I quickly jotted a note to myself reminding me to check Ray's understanding and talk about his language. When I talked to Ray the next day, I shared my observations with him. He quickly replied, "Oh, I know it just means ten and it really isn't ten." In fact, Ray was able to articulate that the tens stick itself wasn't "really" ten but one stick made to look like ten of the units stuck together.

Through our language and practice, we unintentionally establish absolute meaning as we link text and context. In my writing workshop, I have children write vignettes about their lives. This has become a standard part of our work. One day, we were talking about a short play. When I called this a vignette the children were confused. "Is it a true story?" they asked. Through a limited use of the term *vignette*, they had learned only part of its meaning. Our practice had removed the word from its larger context so the children naturally linked vignette to their personal narratives.

The same process applies to mathematics. Many of us, adults and children, have come to understand numbers as absolutes. "4" is four. It is concrete. It is countable. We do not see it as a relative spot on a number line. We forget that infinity exists not only on the positive and negative ends of the number line but in between any two numbers on that line. Integers represent one possible pattern on the line. It happens to be the culturally accepted pattern we learned at a young age by listening to others counting. In another culture, at another time, we might have learned to count this way:

$3\frac{1}{2}, 7, 10\frac{1}{2}, 14, 17\frac{1}{2}\ldots$

Increments of $3\frac{1}{2}$ could have been the standard. Or again, we might have learned to count this way:

one, two, many

Counting is relative to the culture. Numbers exist in relationship to each other and to our need to communicate. Most of us have heard the statement "You're comparing apples and oranges." If the category is fruit, the comparison works. If it is plants, it works. If the category is carbohydrates, it works. If the category is apples, it doesn't work. The same holds true with numbers. Four is more than three, as long as we understand that we are talking about quantity. The comparison breaks down in standards other than simple quantity. We cannot say that four mice are more than three elephants. In this example, consideration of the number of animals renders it true. Thinking of the number of kilograms per group weight, it is not true. The context and purpose determine the response.

My teaching didn't always reflect this. For years, math in my classroom was based predominately on memorization and practice of number patterns and algorithms. Conceptualization, articulation, and investigation were not part of my curriculum. Reduced to mechanical sequence, I was able to teach preplanned lessons, anticipating the result, and recycling children who hadn't mastered the work. But what was missing was meaning. Meaning was left to the individual to determine outside of the context of the classroom.

The number symbolizes something. This correlation to the symbol is the basis of our communication. Teaching children the relative value of numbers allows them to look beyond the numerical representations for meaning. Such critical thinking is especially applicable to our use of graphs and tables. It allows individuals to read and evaluate quantitative information. If adults have this ability, they can make different choices in voting, shopping for food, life insurance, or developing a career.

When we read about Pythagoras' mystical reverence toward mathematics, we see the awe of relationship. The patterns of math and their description of the world fascinated him. Exploration was the factor that motivated. In our culture, as in that established by Pythagoras, we revere numbers. Decisions are made on the basis of numbers. Whether or not to take out a loan, choosing a credit card based on interest rates, or forming an opinion relative to polls indicates the importance of numbers to us. Too often, however, our understanding, and therefore our reverence, is devoted to their absolutes, devoid of relationship. Grading systems and assessments honor "correct" computational derivations. These are cultural perspectives and the math of school is an extension of that culture.

A Tree with Roots: The Mathematics Melting Pot

Our country stands on the shoulders of pioneers and conquistadors. Through perseverance, shrewdness, and power, we have acquired land and built a complex system of government. In little more than two hundred years, we have changed the face of this continent, influenced the culture of the entire world, and threatened the continuance of life as we know it. We occupy a position of prestige and responsibility.

In the process of attaining this position, our means have sometimes been dishonorable. We have forcibly kidnapped people from a distant continent and made them work as slaves. We have completed near genocide on indigenous people. We currently hold third world countries in economic bondage.

"Resistance is futile," say the Borg of Star Trek vintage. Assimilation is their directive. We are like them in many ways. Even as we conquered the people of this continent, we named baseball and football teams, cities, rivers, and mountains after them; a near-posthumous tribute. The conquest did not diminish the fact that we had entered into a relationship with these new cultures. In relationships, everyone is changed. The conquerors are altered by the conquered. The conquered live on in the culture of the conquerors. Alchemists, working with chemical changes in the eleventh century, saw this phenomenon occur in the physical world. They knew that in change, all elements are affected. Volumes of recorded information refer to the alteration and modification of both elements in reaction.

The culture that immigrated across the Atlantic Ocean entered into a relationship with the aboriginal people of North America. In the ensuing years, a river of immigrants came from Europe, with tributaries from Ireland, Italy, and Germany. Each new group brought their culture. The fledgling country became the contact zone of these diverse cultures. The heritage and pride of this country was to welcome the emigres and castaways. Cultures fused and the "melting pot" was born.

This melting pot includes math. It affects us as learners and teachers. We didn't purposely and precisely develop a mathematical system over generations and centuries. We didn't consciously create language and systems to meet our communication needs. Rather, we picked up and accumulated the practices of many cultures along the way. Confusion for our children results from culturally diverse mathematical practices.

Something Old, Anything New?

On Monday morning, children like to tell stories about their weekends. This is a traditional warm-up that we undertake to prepare for writing. For two years, whenever Marco shared, he began with a monologue similar to this:

"On Saturday, no it was Sunday . . . or hmmmmm . . . maybe Saturday."

Marco has a great sense of humor and a wonderful delivery. At first I ignored this stumbling, thinking he was trying to be silly. The children giggled and interrupted him, saying that it didn't matter which day. When none of this stopped Marco's behavior I began to pay closer attention. I wondered why he didn't know. In conversations with him, I realized that keeping days straight was very difficult. Marco was raised in a home where French was the first language he learned. At first I wondered if Marco's difficulty was because English was his second language, yet the very rhythm of days seemed to make no sense to him. Marco made me take a new look at the days of the week. I saw it as a seven-day cycle. Each eighth day, the cycle started over again. Marco didn't understand the base of seven that we use for weeks and months. It was different from the bases he used for other parts of his life.

Our clocks run on a division of a day's length created by Egyptian astronomers in fifteenth century B.C. They noted certain stars that were visible at regular intervals during the night. Extrapolating this to daytime, they divided the cycle into twenty-four "star" units. The sundial developed to mark these units. World travel of later centuries allowed the influence of different cultures to add to thought of the period. It was the influence of the Chinese system of sixty (*knashi*) that added to the clock's development. Twenty-four units (hours) subdivided into sixty units (minutes) subdivided into sixty more units (seconds). All of this came to our culture through Europe. Within the hour, standard clocks emphasize five unit intervals. The face of the standard clock displays two simultaneous systems: twelve hours and sixty minutes. It has the numbers one to twelve written, in between which are five marks. This is the result of the overlay of minutes and hours: sixty divided by twelve equals five. Competent clock users see the "minute hand" at four and know that the four stands for twenty minutes because four sets of five equals twenty. Digital clocks display the numbers one through sixty. Using the same base sixty, they simplify time reading by noting the sixty minute cycle separately and matching the language of time. They start their counting over again at sixty. How do we ask children to find the sense in a system that is complex, having evolved from many different cultures? Christie may pick it up without difficulty, having been asked to read the clock since she was four. Daniel, however, continues to guess with uncertainty. Having to read a double system of hours and minutes eludes him still at ten years old. Compounding the problem is his embarrassment at a lack of skill other children have.

Are there really sixty minutes in an hour? Are there really two sets of twelve hours in a day? (One set of twenty-four in military time.) A slight variation in history might have left us with the time intervals one, two, three, and four. We would count the time between these in fractions or decimals. Or perhaps the day could be divided into one hundred equal sections or hours. The hours could be further divided into one hundred "minutes." It is all a matter of how culture has grown in our particular history. The mathematics of time is an extension of our culture.

Our clock is based on sixty incremental units in sets of twelve, a calendar based on irregular sets of twenty-eight to thirty-one days nested within a set of twelve months. Our monetary system is decimal, ten based with a dollar made up of one hundred pennies, ten dimes, twenty nickels, or four quarters. The quarter itself symbolizes twenty-five hundredths (pennies), but has been given its fractional slang name "quarter" referring to one fourth of a dollar. In our cultural language, a quarter of an hour equals fifteen and a quarter of a dollar equals twenty-five.

Machinists measure in decimals. Map makers measure in miles and their fractions. Carpenters use a system of fractions with the standard foot rooted historically in the measurement of a king's foot. Wood is sold by feet and fractions thereof. Nails are sold by a standard of "penny" weight. Bolts are calibrated decimally. To build a shelf, I may need one by eight (inch) wood, cut in a three-and-a-half-foot length, and fastened with four penny finish nails.

This world of mathematics is confusing to adults, let alone children. It is rooted in culture, not efficiency or sense. In the decade of the seventies, political forces decided it was time to re-educate ourselves and align our mathematical measurement with the rest of the world. Educators were told to prepare their children to enter a world based on the decimal system. Road signs of the future would portray distances in kilometers. Speedometers would measure kilometers per hour and gasoline would be sold in liters. Armed with activities, conversion tables, and objectives, teachers hit the classrooms. What everyone failed to consider was the power of cultural roots. Change is hard and requires much more motivation than mere rational choice for efficiency. Nobody marketed the idea and it soon went bankrupt. Within five years, decimals in measurement were gathering dust in classroom closets.

It is no wonder that Marco was confused. In our culture, the various manifestations of math are not integrated. It is up to the individual to sort out each system and base. When I realized this confusion for Marco, I decided to discuss the big picture with him. Over the next several days, Marco and I explored the various mathematical bases that we use. We started with weeks, drawing several calendar arrays. One had ten by three (Figure 2–1). Another array had six by five. At first fearful of additional confusion, we had to incite his imagination. Through playfulness, Marco began to examine the calendar and compare it to others he created. Marco soon exclaimed, "Oh, I get it!" though he was unable to articulate what he "got." He continued to enjoy the exercise of creating different calendars. With each creation he practiced writing the days of the week in order. The very writing of the days formed a rhythm based on seven for him. He began to "see" the base seven

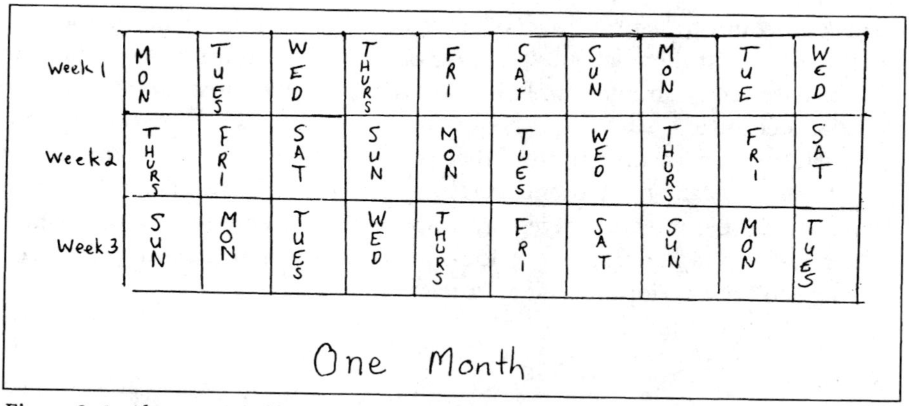

MATHEMATICS AS AN EXTENSION OF CULTURE · 25

Week 1	MON	TUES	WED	THURS	FRI	SAT	SUN	MON	TUE	WED
Week 2	THURS	FRI	SAT	SUN	MON	TUES	WED	THURS	FRI	SAT
Week 3	SUN	MON	TUES	WED	THURS	FRI	SAT	SUN	MON	TUES

One Month

Figure 2–1. *Alternate Weekly Calendar Grid*

in all of his calendar creations. One day, we were joined in discussion by other classmates. Marco explained to them his creations and why, ultimately, the seven day a week calendar worked best. His need to communicate the process and rationale further strengthened his knowledge and sense of the base seven system. I was able to leave the group, discussing and building calendars, so that I could work with other children.

During the next few days, I returned to Marco's group often to present a new context to this work. We talked about and drew clocks. This activity reinforced his work with patterns of five and division. We looked at the twelve-month calendar, money, and rulers, discussing unit and base each time. My lament over the confusion and diversity of these mathematical systems soon turned into a rich source of exploration and investigation into the various cycles, bases, and their histories.

Physiognomy Recapitulates Exogeny

Biologists puzzled over morphological changes in the development of the human fetus from conception to birth. At a given stage, a tail appeared. At another, the fetus appeared to have gills instead of lungs. A theory developed stating that the growth and development of the individual member of the species summarizes characteristics of the growth and development of the species. The individual is a map of the species' development. Genetic encodement was not lost but became part of the chain of growth in the embryo. This theory is summarized in the statement *Physiogomy recapitulates exogeny.*

Could it be that the individual's cognitive growth recapitulates the cognitive stages of the culture? The growth and development of the "body of knowledge" that we share is mirrored in the way that the child learns. Oral language precedes written language. Concrete precedes abstract. A child learns to count to ten on fingers. Ten is the highest number needed for the first few years. It then becomes the foundation of the counting system found in the base ten of Arabic numbers and the Chinese abacus. Cognition recapitulates culture. If we accept this theory, it requires us to acknowledge the importance of allowing the child the space and time to develop concepts. It directs us to teach with patience, trusting children to grow in cognition and concept. Developmental stages are important and should not be rushed. Their mystery should not be overlooked. Each stage is an essential structural support in the development of an integrated mind.

Talk Mathematics to Me

"Look me squarely in the eye and tell me that you left your homework at home?"

"Look, I'm offering you a square deal."

"His ideas of curriculum are very obtuse."

Such phrases become incorporated into our idiomatic speech from geometry. Some of these date to five hundred years before current time. Pythagoreans assigned many values to numbers. One of these values was the representation of justice by the number four and by the square. The square is solid. All sides are equal. To Pythagoras, it was complete. To us a square deal is fair for all parties. Our language today reflects these roots from fourth and fifth century B.C.

Obtuse derives from a Latin word meaning beaten down or blunted. Vernacular definitions have evolved meaning dull or stupid and difficult to understand. An obtuse angle was considered a dull angle, almost imperceptible as an angle and in contrast to a sharp, acute angle. The language of math is rich with etymology. I find that children love the stories that accompany the words.

George Bernard Shaw, a great playwright and essayist, realized that standard English spelling was a jumble. He campaigned to have it reformed into a more sensible system. He left a large sum of money to this end. It has been fifty-nine years since Shaw's death. We still spell the sound "sh" with *sh* or *ti*. Spelling has not changed. Should we lament the mathematical jumble as Shaw did spelling? Or rejoice in the richness of history and geography it carries? How can we help children create sense in this culture?

The Culture of the Classroom

Vivian Paley, a renowned teacher, says, "Even more than the unexamined classroom, I resist the uninvented classroom." Within any classroom, there is a culture. Usually established by the teacher, it can take the form of invention and discovery, discourse, or exposition. Science was one of the first curricular areas to break out of the teacher-directed expository culture. Following the Soviet Union launch of the first satellite, Sputnik, in 1957, panicked National Defense advocates clamored for brighter, more inventive scientific thinking. Programs and texts were organized to encourage children to discover, generalize, and synthesize. No such national emergency catapulted math. Its growth is relatively sluggish, though apparent. Using the standard of Vivian Paley, what might we see in the invented classroom? Could children consider the relative value of numbers? Might scope and sequence be relegated to the recycle bin? Can "math strands" fade?

Pat and I team teach fifty children in the first through sixth grade. Pat principally teaches the younger children; I teach the older group. She came in one morning and suggested that we pose the question "How big is two?" She had no mindset of the outcome of the discussion, but wanted to use it to learn about the children and their thinking. My first assumption was that fourth and fifth graders would state two was simply two and refuse to discuss it. When we have these discussions, I try not to be involved in the content. The older children did indeed first scoff at the notion. They responded immediately.

"It's bigger than one."

"Two what?"

"It depends on what you're counting."

I said nothing. There was silence and expectant looks directed at me. After a short while, Ofer said, "Well, two can be anything." They began to listen to each other and engage in conversation. They wondered if two could be infinitely big. Some were frustrated with the openness of the discussion while others relished it. Besides giving me important information about their thinking, these discussions establish an environment of inquiry in our math workshops. Coupled with sincere listening to children's new discoveries about math, they reinforce a culture where mathematical thinking is honored. I have learned to think carefully about math concepts and to examine areas where I assume absolutes. One such discussion centered around symmetry. Danny had interrupted our art and math exercise to say that absolute symmetry was impossible. At first I ignored this fourth grader who had a history of talking out and challenging class activities. Fortunately, Danny persisted.

"I mean it. There is no perfect symmetry."

"What do you mean, Danny?"

"Well, symmetry can't be exact. It is only an idea."

We stopped and talked as a class. Could things actually be divided into perfectly mirrored halves? Children gave examples of leaves and butterflies. Each time, Danny, with a growing number of followers, refuted the claim. In the end, many of us were convinced that symmetry was an idea and actual things only came close to it. For the next two years, Danny made our class aware of this. It became part of our culture to talk precisely about symmetry.

A fictitious character in our classroom culture is "Momo." Momo always presents a math dilemma to consider. One year, the children entered into a friendly banter with me. They urged me to send Momo away. According to them, the math dilemmas would leave with Momo. On a Monday, they decided that Momo was going to Mexico to visit family. I readily gave them permission to send Momo away, asking only that they be specific about cousins, calculate distance, and learn about this new place. We were able to give new life to this part of the culture through their invention. Momo kept in contact for the rest of the year, describing relatives, animals, and holidays in Mexico. We practiced counting in Spanish, compared the states in Mexico to those in the United States and graphed the population of Mexico City to that of Los Angeles, Portland, and our own Ashland.

The Culture of the Child

I was at Marco's conference. He had chosen to share multiplication work from his math log with his parent. There were a lot of algorithms scattered around the page. I asked him to explain his work on one problem to his mother. The problem follows.

```
    24
    24         24          24
    24         24         x 13
    24         24          144
    24         24         + 68
    24         24          202
    24         24
  + 24       + 24
    68        144
```

He began to explain. "It says thirteen groups of twenty-four. So I wrote thirteen twenty-fours. I wrote it in two groups, then I added it up. I got two hundred and two. It's right because four groups of twenty-four is like a hundred. So thirteen . . . wait a minute . . . that can't be right."

Marco's parent knew the importance of allowing him time to think and process new information. He sat for a minute, then finished.

"If every four groups is a hundred, the answer must be more. Like around three hundred. Wait. I think I did something wrong here."

Marco was a fifth grade student. He had an individual education plan in math because assessments demonstrated that he had a learning disability. In fact, learning multiplication facts was nearly impossible. Creating strategies was difficult. Surprisingly though, Marco could estimate answers. He was often correct. I had to be especially attentive to catch his talk because he didn't trust his estimations. When asked to think about one or explain how he arrived at it, he became flustered and filled with self-doubt. He was apologetic. I concluded that, since the learning of algorithms was very difficult for Marco, he assumed that the path to the correct answer was arduous. He thought that his method was too easy to be correct. Yet, somehow, without using cumbersome algorithms or applying mathematical laws, Marco could solve these problems. Could it be that the culture of math in my classroom obscures the individual's ability to interact mathematically with the world?

While living in the dominant social culture in which we find ourselves, each of us develops an individual culture. This is a set of values, norms, and behaviors that determine the way we will respond in a given situation. This individual culture is our personal history. Knowing an individual's culture allows me to understand their view of the world and to speak in the language of their mind. It has taken me years to cultivate the behavior of listening to a child earnestly in order to learn the language and culture of their mind.

I try to diminish the space between myself and the child to create the relationship of learning. This is difficult or impossible if I am afraid of the content of math or feel insecure about my mastery of it. It took a slight shift in perception and attitude to realize that the most important content is the child's individual language and culture. The child is the map maker and user. It is my goal to understand the map and help the child to revise when they recognize the need and make the choice.

A close friend of mine has a son named Tim. A very insightful child, he had a distinct personal culture at a young age. Tim provided us with many lessons.

He was a few weeks into his first school experience when one morning, Tim's brothers found their mother in the kitchen and announced, "You'd better go check on Tim. He's at it again."

She found Tim in his bedroom. He was repeating "Five and two. Five and two."

"What is it?" his mother asked. "What do you mean, five and two?"

"Five days to do their thinkings and only two to do mine. It isn't fair."

Tim had learned the pattern of school culture and was questioning it. He much preferred to stay home and "do" his own thinkings. What is it that allowed Tim to understand this rhythm when other children don't know it in fifth grade? Some children ask, "Is tomorrow school?" What is the culture of the child? How can we help to develop it?

While some children in my class need to "do their own thinking," others long for math workbooks. When I first began to consider the importance of children's construction of concepts and meaning, I balked at workbooks. They dictated a child's development. I felt as though children's desire for workbooks threatened constructive development. I considered this desire to be a result of behavioral habits and expectations developed in previous classrooms and through media exposure. It wasn't until I felt comfortable and confident in my work with math constructivism that I was able to step back from the situation. At that point, I wanted to understand the children's desire. I began to allow children to play with workbooks and found that the workbooks were just one more tool for math. Now when I come across discards or extras, I keep them around. I also have math textbooks near the manipulatives on the math shelves. I often find that by October, many of the math books have left the shelf and found residence in students' desks. Some children ask me how to use them. I conference with individuals and sometimes give a whole class lesson about the format and reading of texts. Some children take them home and work with them. The interest wanes, however, and is replaced by interaction, conversation, and discovery during math workshop. This is what I care about and what I plan for during math. I see myself as part of an interactive culture, a co-creator with the children. Since I have access to materials and spend more time than they do in the classroom, my influence is strong. As part of the culture, I respect that influence by continuing to be interested in mathematical thinking and strategies, excited about new discoveries involving math made by the children or me. It is important for children to see their team of teachers involved in solving math problems, considering new ideas, and discussing concepts. Individual mathematical inquiry is a fundamental part of our culture. We don't just model it, we try to live it. Our math inquisitiveness and passion is transmitted to our children.

The Culture of Mathematics Education

"Take out your workbooks and look at page sixty-three."

"First you add the ones column. Then add the tens column."

"Know those multiplication tables."

Tests, quizzes, calculators, pattern blocks, tens blocks—anthropologists define ancient cultures by the implements and patterns of movement that they find. We leave trails. As teachers of mathematics, we are defined by the implements and practices that we bring to our classroom. What is the culture of mathematic education?

Pat and I presented a workshop to a group of teachers on conversation within math as a way to involve children in thinking mathematically. We chose to organize the workshop in the same way we organize a math workshop with our children. We talked about fundamental questions such as: How big is two? How big is infinity? At the end of an hour and a half, one teacher approached me to ask, "Do other teachers at your school think like you?"

I hadn't thought about the thinking of other teachers at my school, but it seemed some did and some didn't. I replied, "The others in my team share these beliefs but it takes constant awareness and work to construct our own thinking."

"I like what you're saying and I believe you, but the other teachers in my school think only in terms of rules and algorithms. They expect children leaving my class to know these rules, so I am afraid to take time for much else."

It is very difficult to teach in isolation though many teachers have been practicing alone for years. In the sixties and seventies, Herb Kohl talked of taping artwork over his doorway window, keeping the door closed, and teaching the way he knew he must. Not only can the particular culture of mathematics education at our school keep us from developing strategies with children, it can keep us personally from thinking of new strategies. The time and effort we put into each act, like covering the window of our door, decreases the time and effort we are able to put into thinking. We must begin in education to create a culture of inquiring learners among the staff of our school. Within this culture, math inquiry, thoughtfulness, and conversation will grow. Albert Einstein wrote, "Only in an atmosphere of freedom can a mind function fully."

3

Watch Your Language

Gratiano speaks an infinite deal of nothing, more than any man in all Venice. His reasons are as two grains of wheat hid in two bushels of chaff: you shall seek all day ere you find them, and when you have them, they are not worth the search.

—SHAKESPEARE
Merchant of Venice

The language we use in instruction and assignment is chosen to assist children in understanding, and is used to clarify and elucidate concepts and direction. However, this language is often based on our prior knowledge of not only the content, but the path of learning children will take. It is easy for us to assume that children understand our words and phrases. We believe they will follow our thought process to begin their work. Their confusion often confuses and frustrates us. We must watch our language if we want children to be successful in math.

Children's language informs our work. They reveal themselves in language. Through careful observation we can learn what they hear, how they process our language, and whether or not they have an inner voice. To discover this, we must listen and then listen again. Our questions become more important than our answers.

You Can't Take Eight Away from Two

As a young, new teacher I prided myself on my math skills. Algebra, geometry, trigonometry, and calculus had been easy for me and I expected, under my enlightened guidance, math to be the same for my third grade students. I planned enthusiastic lessons and my explanations were energetic. A favorite tactic of mine arose when Daniel approached me with his solution to this problem:

$$\begin{array}{r} 242 \\ -138 \\ \hline 116 \end{array}$$

Daniel had made an error common to members of the class. Not employing regrouping, or as I called it, "borrowing," he had simply reordered the problem to suit his ability to solve it. He had subtracted two from eight. Ready as always, I jumped to the rescue. First we read the problem. Then I imperatively stated, "You can't take eight away from two." A look of bewilderment and confusion passed over Daniel's face so I continued.

"Daniel, do you have any money?"

"No."

"Well what if I ask you to give me eight dollars?"

"I can't."

"What if you have two dollars? Can you give me eight?"

"No."

"There you have it! Now you could borrow from Justin if he has money, right?"

"Yeah."

"Suppose Justin only has a ten dollar bill and he was willing to lend it to you. You could then give me eight and have two dollars left. Do you understand?"

"Yeah."

"Okay, pretend the four in this problem is Justin's four ten dollar bills. Borrow one of them. How many does Justin have?

"Three."

"Right, and you have ten plus this two. How much do you have?"

"Twelve."

"Good. Let's record that transaction."

I felt like such a successful teacher. Daniel understood borrowing. Or did he? Over time, I noticed that children would make the same mistake again and again. My self-assurance and enthusiasm led children to mask their confusion and feel isolated in it. Reviewing this style of teaching, I realized that I was imposing the sense I made out of math onto Daniel. What was Daniel saying inside his head when I didn't take the time to listen?

Even if Daniel internalized my thinking and strategies, in the long run it was counter productive. You *can* take eight away from two. This is the foundation of our entire economy. From credit cards to house loans to the national debt, we operate in the realm of negative numbers. Calculating our ability to enter debt and pay it off is an important skill in our society. If Daniel were to accept and believe my language that "You can't take eight away from two," he would have a difficult time understanding his personal finances in later life.

Besides that, in my example, Daniel still owed Justin money. It wasn't the same as adjusting the place value within a number while conserving the number value. My strategy could only be useful in that it had drama and a story that might trigger the algorithmic process for Daniel the next time he encountered such a problem.

    Years later, as I learned to listen to and watch children, Adam taught me a new way of thinking. By now I was teaching in a first through fifth grade multiage program. Math workshop was filled with manipulative materials, predominately tens blocks. Adam was trying to solve a similar equation. I asked him to explain his work on the following problem.

$$\begin{array}{r} 141 \\ -39 \\ \hline 110 \end{array}$$

$$\begin{array}{r} 110 \\ -8 \\ \hline 102 \end{array}$$

    "Well, first I took thirty away from one hundred and forty. I knew in my mind that that left one hundred and ten. Then I still had to use the nine. When I took nine away from one I ended up with a negative eight. I had to put that together with the one hundred and ten. I knew I had to count down to do this. So I got one hundred and two."

    This problem demonstrates an understanding of the numeric value of one hundred forty-one. The process Adam used to solve this problem and his explanation shows that he was able to conserve the value of the original number, one hundred forty-one, throughout his work. Did Adam's way show greater understanding than the traditional algorithm? Should I use this method to teach these problems? No. What I have learned by listening to children in math workshop is that if I don't rush to impose my thinking and if I provide an environment rich in time, material, interaction, and consideration, the children will develop many accurate strategies. In addition, through the culture of the classroom, children observe and discuss each other's strategies. When the children find a new one that looks attractive, they explore it.

What Do You Mean You're Talking to the Wall?

Joe came to us in February of his first grade year. He had been in a class in our school that was giving the teacher a challenge. The principal decided to split the "difficult" children into different classes. Joe was labeled as the most difficult. My partner teacher, Pat, had worked as a speech and language teacher and was often pointing out how our language confused children.

One day, after Joe had a particularly disruptive time in class standing on a desk and cussing at Pat, she took him into the hall to talk. During this conversation, Joe was looking around, and as was typical, he was carrying on a conversation of his own.

"Joe, I feel like I'm talking to the wall here."

Joe immediately looked up with keen interest.

"What do you mean, you're talking to the wall? Why would anyone talk to a wall?"

Pat burst out laughing at her own language. Joe may have had difficulty with understanding and complying with behavior norms, but he knew the purpose of spoken language was to convey meaning. He often pointed out the irony of our unconsidered words. Language, rich in double meaning and cultural influence, can leave children confused if we don't take the time to check their understanding.

The Rise and Fall of the Gozzindas

Math gozzindas derive from our talk about division. Given the simple problem:

$$4\overline{)12}$$

teachers, including me, read this as how many times does four go into twelve. The answer, reflecting our language, would be four goes into twelve three times. It wasn't until I was sitting at a parent/teacher conference with Becky that I learned how students might hear this language. We were discussing what goals Becky would undertake during the winter of her third grade year. She piped up with, "I think I should learn my gozzindas." I was baffled. Completely content with her idea, Becky didn't go on to explain.

"Tell me what you mean by gozzindas, Becky."

"You know. That math stuff. Like four gozzinda twelve."

Becky's parent and I chuckled over this mistaken rendition of the phrase. But something about it kept haunting me. If Becky could believe that the language of math was completely different from the language she uses regularly, then she wouldn't see the connection of her math work to her description of and communication about the world. Math language became foreign; a language spoken only in classrooms. I began looking at the rest of my language in math. What did I mean by "times"? Was this a math term or a term children used in the course of describing experiences in life? What about "plus"? Understanding the importance of connecting the language of math to the language of children, I went to the playground, notebook in hand to listen.

"You've already had four turns (on the swings)."
"Well, you were on three times."
"We get Michelle (on our team)."
"No way. You already have more."
"How many times do I have to tell you?"

The playground was abundant with math language. How could I bring it into the classroom and bridge the gap between playground math language and classroom math language? I refined my list to words that could bridge this gap and began a series of classroom discussions about math and language. These included times, more than, into, and fair. Simply by reporting my observations and letting children discuss them from their perspective, we were able to introduce a new understanding of language both on the playground and in the classroom.

Deliberate Creation of Problems

One of the first things I realized I needed to change was the language of problems. Trying to create equity in physical activities and problem genres, I couldn't avoid sexist comments and competition among the children in my class. Gender-laden names either led to questions of problem authenticity or my attempts at reversing assumptions. My partner teacher was way ahead of me. She had been using "Momo" as the main character in problem building for a number of years. Without the use of personal pronouns, Momo could always be either boy or girl. Occasionally this caused children to wonder, but it avoided stereotypical roles. During the past few years, Momo has ridden a bike across town, visited cousins in Mexico, surveyed lunch choices in the cafeteria and collected RBIs in baseball. Momo's family also enters our problems. We solve problems for Mimi, Roro, and Jojo.

The other major factor in establishing our problems is the realism involved in the concept and solution. The math we encounter on a daily basis involves a constellation of strategies. Problem generation includes consideration of a spectrum of math operations and strategies. We might use a problem like the one following.

> Momo's class was joining three other classes for a field trip. This added up to one hundred five children (105). There were four teachers and five parents participating in the field trip. If a bus can hold forty-eight (48) people, how many buses will be needed for this trip?

Another might be:

> Mimi's class was studying bread. They had a bread recipe and wanted to attempt making it. The children wanted to make enough so that every

three would have a loaf. The recipe called for two eggs per loaf. There are thirty (30) children in class. The teacher was going to the store to buy eggs for this project. How many dozens of eggs were needed?

There are many steps in solving these problems. In math workshop, children will employ a variety of strategies including pictures, diagrams, and numeric patterns. Besides observing these, we look for sense in the final solution. Will children decide they need two buses with eighteen left over? Will they opt for three buses? Will they reason that so much wasted space is not very respectful of resources and suggest that some people follow the buses in cars?

In the egg problem, will they decide the teacher needs to buy two and one half dozen eggs? Will they realize the need for three dozen? Will they ask a grocer to split a set? The key to these problems is reason. We want children to follow mathematical strategies to solve them, but we want the solution to make sense according to their knowledge of the world. In fact, we want to broaden their understanding of how they can interact with their world.

Still, there are aspects of these problems that can create difficulty. In the egg problem, we assume that children know that a dozen eggs equals twelve. They have to work on two levels, repeating the pattern of two eggs per loaf and then converting this number into sets of twelve. Anticipation of children's responses is not always possible, but it is important for me to attempt this each time. Sometimes when I present a problem I watch to see if the language is interfering. Sometimes, knowing it will be a challenge, I look for strategies children use to understand the language.

Who Uses Quotient?

I attended a district math curriculum meeting recently. One teacher in particular was intent on chastising elementary-school teachers for not properly preparing children for middle school. When asked what was missing, she had a number of responses. First, children were too dependent. They didn't sit down with a problem and begin experimenting with strategies. Upon presenting the problem, this teacher was besieged with questions. These children had been promoted without self-confidence, according to her.

I would certainly agree with the need for children to approach problems with confidence, but I think we need to listen to their worries. What kinds of questions are the children asking? Do they reflect the language of the problems? Are the children able to process the language in order to sort out the concepts? What is the class make-up? In cross-graded classes, I notice that young, new students are hesitant.

In addition, this teacher complained that children did not know the language of algorithms. They were not able to identify quotients, dividends, addends, products, and so forth. I wonder about this language. How does it fit into their acquisition of language in general? In current vernacular, a product is the concrete end result of a process. It is what comes out of a production line. Can this relate to the product in a multiplication problem? Perhaps we can discuss the product as the end of a series of repeated addition numbers. But what about quotient? Its origins are from the Latin word for "how many." Does anybody use this term to describe the world? Will teaching its origin help make it meaningful? What actually is a dividend besides a check stock market investors receive each quarter? This word is derived from the Latin word for "widow." It refers to the separation caused by death. Our understanding of these words will allow us to teach the language of algorithms within context.

The Language of Help

Most of us have children with varying degrees of limitation in our classes. This year, I have Louis, who has been diagnosed with autism. I am always fascinated by the reactions of adults to Louis. Louis operates at a high functional level. His capabilities in math elude my understanding. He struggles with counting past twenty-nine, but can memorize in isolation a number of facts. He can compute multiplication, addition, and subtraction problems with numbers and solutions higher than he can count.

Sometimes caring adults unwittingly hinder learning. This seems to be what happened to Louis. My ninety-minute math workshop always begins with a group gathering to consider a concept and set the stage for the day's work. When students leave the group gathering, they have a problem to explore. The first step of the work sets up the process that children will employ for their first attempt at the problem. Some will move to their desks with their math log and begin working independently, others will move to the shelves with the manipulatives on them, some will form small groups to discuss the problem, and some will sit and plan their strategies. I learn a great deal from watching these first few minutes of math workshop. I use the information to direct my work for the day and to talk to the children about their first steps in problem solving.

I noticed that a parent helper, educational assistant, or resource teacher went to help direct Louis at the beginning of each workshop. Caring for him, and being concerned that the instruction and directions might be overwhelming to him, these adults were acting out of their best interest for Louis. But I couldn't help wondering if this action was the best for him. Louis was being taught helplessness. After the first few weeks, I asked people to leave him alone and see what would happen. Hard as it was, everyone managed. Louis would wait for a while for the help and then would either come to an adult or begin math work. Curious to see how Louis sought help, I watched and listened. At first he would thrust his math log at someone and say, "I don't know what to do."

I began working with the adults and with Louis to help him learn the language of asking for help. I wanted him to have options and skills for getting help. Through questions, we started working to develop his inner voice to express what he wanted. Some of his questions and statements developed as follows:

"This is too hard, will you give me something easier?"
"I know what I'm supposed to do, but I don't get . . ."
"Can I just use a calculator?"
"Will you help me with the tens blocks?"

Whatever Louis learns in math, the ability to articulate his need for help is most important for him. He will use this skill well beyond our work together. Louis will teach others to listen instead of assuming they know his needs. In our program, we refer to individuals with special needs as our "indicator species." This is because what is good for them is good for everyone. Conversely, what is difficult for them is difficult for others. These children inform us about the classroom environment. Through this work with Louis, I realized that I didn't spend enough time with the children teaching them how and when to ask for help. The language that Louis learned was nothing different from the language that each child needs in talking to each other and to their teachers.

I Can't Do My Plus Threes

A group of students sat outside the door of a classroom with a "closed" sign on it before school one morning. One child was working on a paper with math problems. Their discussion began as follows:

Brittany asked, "What are you doing?"
"My threes," explained Aaron.
"Haven't you passed them?"
"No, I can't do my threes."

I was curious about this self-declaration. Having talked to Aaron's previous teacher, I knew that he had been competent and confident in math during first and second grade. When I asked him about not being able to "do threes" he replied that he couldn't pass the timed test. It seemed that math assessment in his school career had changed from concept construction and problem solving to speed and accuracy. Both are important and teachers decide which is their first priority regularly during their curriculum planning. The important point for us is to help children sort out and identify what they can and can't do. Exactly which part of the work gives Aaron difficulty? What skills does he need to develop so he can become proficient?

In the fall, many of my former students drop by after school to visit. I ask them how school is going, what they are studying, and if they are struggling with anything. Jadyn returned in September and reported that middle school was good but math was very hard. He was having trouble. Immediately I began to wonder where I had gone wrong. Having worked with Jadyn for three years, I thought he was quite competent in math. So I asked him what the struggle was with math.

"It's too hard," Jadyn explained.

"What is it that makes math hard?" I asked.

"Their problems are really hard."

"Do you have trouble solving the problems?"

"Oh, no," Jadyn clarified. "That's easy. It's just that I have to solve between twenty-five and fifty every night."

I was relieved. Hard for Jadyn meant something entirely different than it did for me. Hard was the tedious and time-consuming repetitive work for Jadyn. I would have assumed it meant conceptually and strategically difficult.

By December all of my students had come by to visit except Joel. Joel had been particularly eager to leave the halls of elementary school for bigger and better things. He had also been an exceptional math student. During his fourth and fifth grade years, Joel consumed problems. He loved solving equations more than articulating his thinking in story problems but was competent in both. He had developed tactics to solve many problems including multiplication and division of fractions. Joel was an expert in using diagrams to check problems. With two days of school left before winter vacation, I spotted the shuffle coming down the hall that I had come to know as Joel's. After a sheepish greeting, we began catching up on his family and school life. Finally, I got to the subject of math.

"How is math?"

"Okay, but hard."

"What do you mean?"

"I think you should teach it differently."

"What should I do differently?"

"Well, first of all, give lots of homework," Joel asserted.

"You've got a lot of homework?" I asked, still trying to understand why Joel was struggling.

"Yeah. And you need to use a math book."

"Why?"

"The book was hard at first. I didn't get it."

As we talked, it turned out that the work in the book was easy for Joel, but reading the text and sorting out the language was hard. I borrowed a book from the middle school to see if I could understand the problem Joel had encountered. Unlike the language we had developed in our program, the math book was written by adults. With children in mind, they used bright pictures depicting talking and interacting. Shown are current topics of environment and politics. The actual ratio of problem to text averages less than 10 percent. The challenge for the child is to separate the language and diagrams used to attract them from the language of instruction and problem. This is a major challenge for some children and can cause otherwise mathematically competent children to doubt themselves. The authenticity of an individual child or class building their own mathematical content according to current information in their lives is lost. Following Joel's advice, I pull out math texts and have class discussions. We explore the format and search for context meaning. Children compare the assignments to our work and learn to decipher the text.

Groups of or *Into Groups*

Eve was an intense child. She required a lot of time to process information and she demanded an understanding of concepts. She took very little at face value. She learned early on that any timed assessment would fail her, so she quit trying. She would argue at length, often reaching the point of tears. Her argument was not intended to prove herself right, but to demonstrate the beliefs and concepts that were keeping her from embracing something new. In this, Eve taught me a great deal. I knew immediately when my language was unclear or contained wrong assumptions about children's thinking. Often when working with Eve in math I could see frustration building in her eyes, so I would ask her to take a break and draw or walk to the library. My intent was to remove the pressure that was locking her into resistance.

One of the greatest lessons Eve taught me concerned division. I had been using manipulatives to demonstrate the relationship between division and a repeated series of subtraction. In this, the problem

$$18\overline{)144}$$

would be read as one hundred forty-four divided into groups of eighteen. The question I asked was, How many groups would there be? Children usually take one hundred forty-four items (buttons, cubes, base ten blocks) and remove one group of eighteen at a time until they have removed as many items as they can. I ask them to record the steps of their work and they demonstrate a model similar to one shown in Figure 3–1.

Eve was having a great deal of trouble. None of this made sense to her. Something inside her rebelled every time we approached the first step of the problem. After several tries during one week, I asked Pat, my partner teacher,

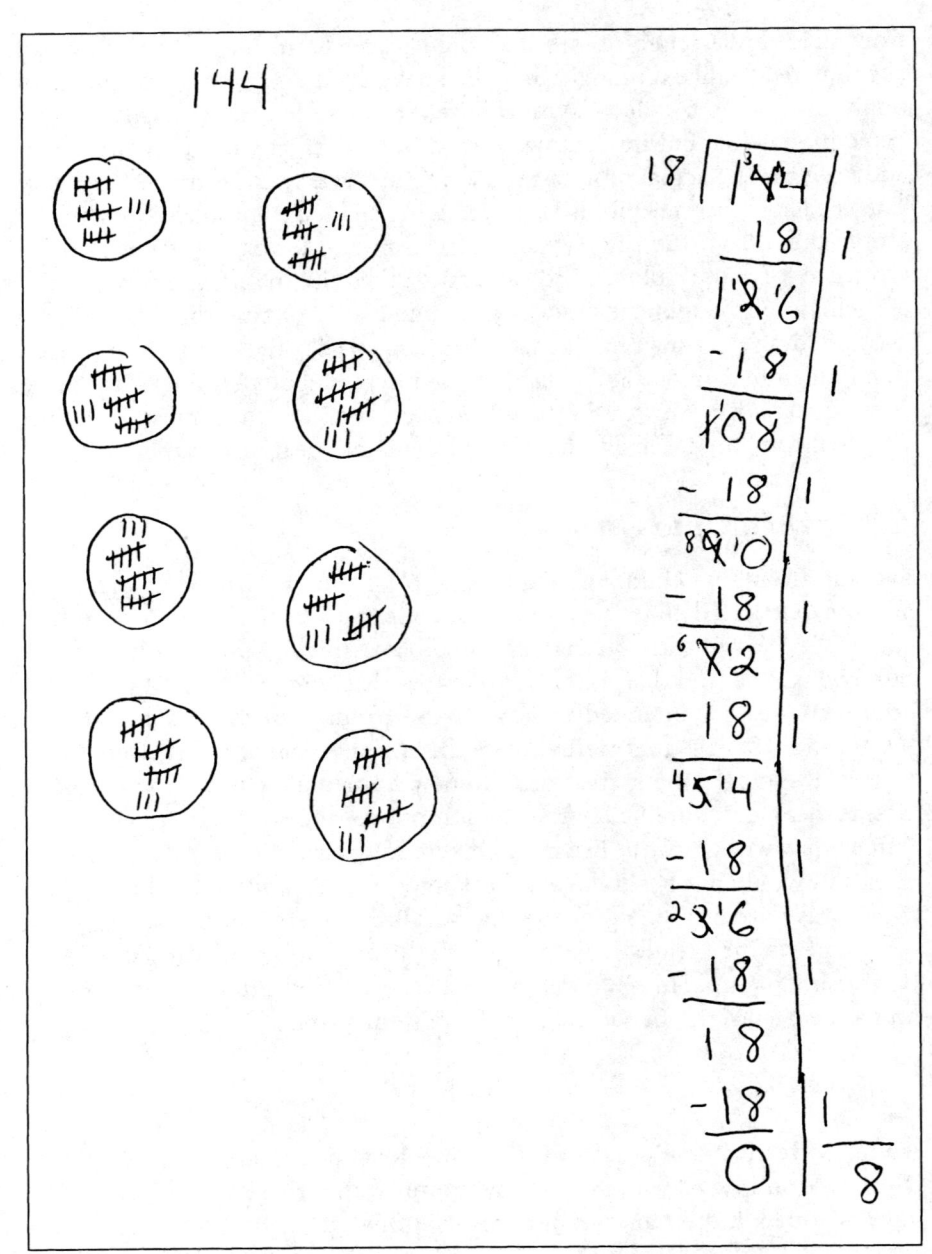

Figure 3–1. *Division Problem*

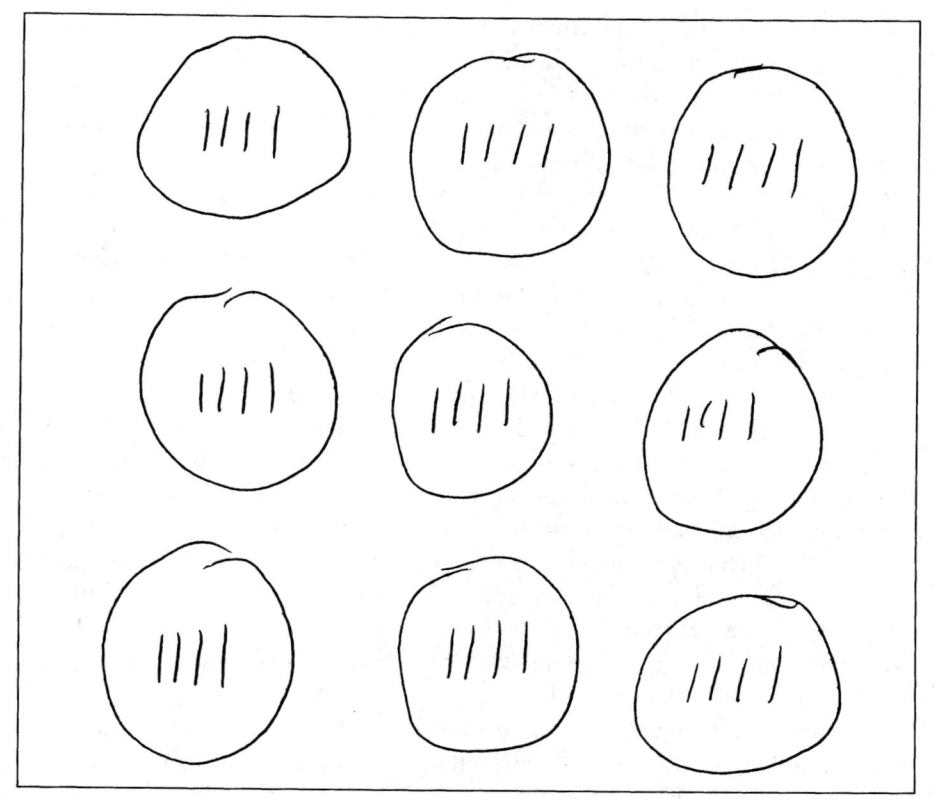

Figure 3–2. Division Problem

if we could discuss Eve's struggle. As we shared stories of Eve's math work, it became obvious that division should not create difficulty for her. She was competent. She had been able to divide numbers in third grade. We finally decided to create a time when she could revisit Pat, her third grade teacher, to investigate this division. I reviewed my division process with Pat, emphasizing the repeated subtraction.

After spending a half hour with Eve, Pat had the answer. Eve had learned the concept of division differently. When faced with the problem

$$9\overline{)36}$$

Eve could easily work it. Her strategy was to make nine circles and fill them equally using up the thirty-six (Figure 3–2).

Eve, through her struggle, was demonstrating the difference Pat and I used in our language. Pat had taught children that the division problem $9\overline{)36}$ meant thirty-six divided into nine equal groups. My language assumed the interpretation of thirty-six divided into equal groups of nine. The result (quotient) would yield the same answer: *four* in each of nine groups or *four* groups of nine. The answer of four could be derived either way.

The difference in process had to do with the commutative law of multiplication being applied to division through missing factors (4 x 9 = 36 or 9 x 4 = 36). But more importantly, this situation led us to new reflection on our teaching. We were amazed that no one before Eve had demonstrated confusion from the difference in our language. Had they understood the relationships of factors and derived the law without saying anything? Had they simply allowed their mind to separate into Tim's way and Pat's way? Or perhaps they decided that some kind of quantum change occurred when division was carried out with larger numbers or when they moved into fourth grade.

No matter what children had done to compensate for these differences, we learned something important for our teaching. Many more lunch times were devoted to our understanding of division. I worked problems using Pat's language as she worked with mine. We discussed the ramifications of using both languages in each classroom. We attempted to apply the language to actual math problems that needed solving. In the end, we realized that the language of the problem needed to match the language of the solution. Isolated into abstract numbers it didn't matter, but if I wanted to seat thirty-six people for a workshop and wanted to seat them into groups of nine, I would have a different arrangement than if I wanted to seat them into nine equal groups. The strategy must correlate to the question. The important lesson was to use both languages with the children and to ask that their answers demonstrate whether they are talking about *groups of* or *into groups*.

Four Point Five

I had a number of division problems on the board. One of these was eighty-one divided by eighteen. I asked the children to solve the problem and prove that their answer was correct. I was working with a few of the students when Ryan caught my attention.

"My answer can't be right."

"Why not?"

"Because the calculator says that the answer is four point five."

"I see. Why does that make your answer wrong?"

"Well, see I had four and a half."

Somehow, children learn to read a decimal as "point." This practice seems to be a common linguistic short cut with older children and adults. But in elementary school, the gap between the meaning of a decimal and the language of "point" becomes too wide for understanding. The language detracts from understanding.

I have learned that spending time reading decimals with care to the language of place value makes for an easy transition between decimals and fractions. Considered language helps children to be able to develop strategies for solving problems involving decimals. The same is true with reading other types of problems. The time we take as a class to read math benefits us by developing the common understanding and vocabulary. It enables us to work together. We read equations, fractions, geometry, division, multiplication, and subtraction problems regularly in our group meeting before math workshop begins.

The Language of Assessment Tools

Years ago, I took a workshop from author and educator Herb Kohl. His theme was that teachers needed to be their own authority. Besides outlining his priorities in teaching, he talked about techniques we might use to ensure our sovereignty in the classroom. One of these techniques involved the state assessment tests. Herb believed that we knew what to teach and how to teach a particular community of learners. The assessment was independent of the authentic planning and assessment cycle that occurs with teachers. His idea was to teach as we know how. When the assessment was about to be given, quietly close the classroom door and teach a unit on test-taking skills and vocabulary to the class. Allow them to understand and explore the difference between math workshop and the test prior to actual work on the test.

The underlying problem that Kohl was addressing is that standardized tests are not geared to assess an individual's progress. They operate on a grosser level to compare counties, districts, schools, and children. In this comparison, they seek common ground in math language as well as the language of directions and problem setup. Even with current NCTM standards, state assessment reforms, and classroom-based assessment, it looks as if these standard assessments are here to stay. Achievement scores may impact individual children. Therefore, teachers must look at them seriously.

Our state sends out sample tests accompanied by scoring guides and benchmark standards. I use the sample test questions to teach children how to read these particular mathematical assessments. We discuss the language of the question and the inner voice that will help children with this task. Take, for example, this problem from a test sample:

> Monica wants to put tile on her kitchen floor. Her kitchen is perfectly square. One side of the kitchen is 9 feet. Each tile is 1 square foot. How many tiles does she need to cover the entire floor?
>
> a. 9
> b. 27
> c. 81
> d. There's no way to tell.

In learning to solve this problem, children need to sort out and conserve pertinent information and discard superfluous content and information. Addressing a problem like this as a group allows individuals to share their approach, articulate their inner voice, listen to others, and evaluate the efficiency of their thinking. Test-taking approaches in my class include looking at the answers and discarding obviously incorrect answers. Adam is quick to point out that there have to be more than nine tiles. Eve wants help visualizing the problem. Classmates point out the sentence of the square. Still confused, Eve wonders why that is important. Not until Ryan suggests that Eve draw a picture of the floor in her head and then asks her to describe the floor does Eve begin to fill in the important detail. I hope that through this dialogue, Eve and other children will begin to learn how they might ask themselves questions.

On another day, I was interested in working with Sonja and Claire regarding their multiplication strategies. I pulled out the sample of "Open-Ended Math Questions" from the state assessment and chose a problem I thought the children could successfully develop. The problem follows:

> Mrs. Newhouse is beginning an exercise program. She plans to walk 2 miles for 2 days, 3 miles for 3 days, 4 miles for 4 days, and continue the pattern until she is walking 6 miles per day. In how many days will she first walk 6 miles? Explain your thinking at each step and your answer.

My planning had evolved around the time I would spend with Sonja and Claire. After our opening work, I read and distributed the problem and asked children to work on it while I held a mini workshop with the two girls. We had no sooner started our work that I noticed the noise level in the room rise above simple discussion. Suppressing the tendency to rebuke them for their behavior, I listened. It was obvious there was some confusion about the problem. I asked three children close by what was wrong. They replied that they couldn't tell if Mrs. Newhouse walked one mile each day for two days totaling two miles or if she walked two miles each day totaling four miles. They were trying to set up a t-chart to solve the problem and could not get direction from the problem's language. Calling the class back together again, I saw that the children expressed anger and frustration with the problem. They could not predict the author's intent. I explained that I had assumed that she walked two miles each day for two days and that I probably would have guessed it stated that. We discussed clear language in the setup of math problems.

I learned the importance of suspending my skills in reading a problem the way the writer meant it. Assessment tests assume that children understand the language. Instead, I have to read the problem the way children read it. This means anticipating possible interpretations that children may have.

How will the child with processing difficulty read it? How will the child who anticipates difficulty with problem solving read it?

Ground Those Problems in the World

Ted owns a local landscape business. I asked him to come into class and work with the children on our Native Plant Park Project. He helped us prepare for a major planting day. In explaining the importance of the preparation for planting, Ted said, "Remember, a five-dollar plant should be placed in a fifty-dollar hole." What did Ted mean by this? Was it pertinent to math? Was it worth discussing? I decided to ask the children what Ted meant. Some of them understood this axiom, while others had no idea. They talked about the importance of patient work and careful planning in creating an environment for the plants. I introduced the language of investment and long-term benefits.

Sometimes I wonder if I put this same maxim to use in my preparation for math. The time and care with which I create the problem will pay off in the quality of the workshop that develops. To that end, specific problems need to be created for each class according to the corporate ability and culture of the group. Sometimes these problems succeed immensely and sometimes they fail miserably. Failure is part of the experiment. It provides us with valuable information. Children will face ambiguous language. It is part of our culture. Learning to identify unclear language and predict an author's intent is an important skill.

Recently, we were figuring out ways to collect and organize data, create summary statements, and display information. Students were familiar with surveys and information sorting. We had been referring to books children were reading to derive language discussions. It seemed to follow naturally that we might look in books to gather statistics for this math focus. Pat and I posed a simple question to the children: What are the five most common words in the English language? Our idea was that the children would consider where to look for their information, organize a collection system, and go to work. We imagined them creating a chart and looking through books.

The primary class explored this question first. Children worked orally to understand the language of the problem. They asked questions. What is meant by "common words"? How can we determine a "common word"? As we anticipated, they considered and discussed where this information might be located. Some of them decided to survey other children asking, "What do you think are the most common words?" Others decided to look in books. Most formulated a hypothesis and went to work trying to support it. The workshop broke down with the problem of sorting and organizing information. How could they keep track of common words? There were too many. How could they separate individual words into common or not common? Had we given them five or six words and asked them to determine which are more common, they would have known how to proceed. With their fascination with words and language, the problem motivated them, but was too open.

We posed the same problem with our older children. These fourth and fifth graders had more experience with data collection. When given the problem, they talked a bit and eagerly set to work. Much to our surprise, however, the idea of words common to language spread through the group and was adopted by all. Within minutes, survey sheets were set up and the classroom was buzzing. The question of the day seemed to be "What five words do you use the most?" Children had fun with the notion. Words emerged like "cool," "duh," and "Tim." When we regrouped, I led a discussion.

"How do you know that these are most common to the English language?"

"We checked," Ricky replied.

Chloe added, "These are the ones we use the most."

"But the English language refers to all English *speakers* and *users*. Not just our class," I countered.

They became confused and frustrated. Even when an assistant in the room suggested that they turn to books, children resisted. While the younger children had been willing to look at "standard" language, these children were more interested in the language that they thought important: The language they used in their social interaction.

Our question had been set up to assess their ability to develop data collection and organization. It seemed simple enough. What we missed, however, was their world. We didn't anticipate the relationship each class and age group had with language. In cases like these, the assessment turns right around and faces us. It is the problem that is assessed. We have to evaluate our sophistication in presenting a problem that would be grounded in their world.

Money problems are always useful to me. By listening to and watching the class, I can find many ways to extend and apply their concepts. In the fall of 1997, Spawn toys and Gigapets found their way into the classroom. Distractions that irritated me also became a rich source of math. It seemed almost everyone in class knew the cost of either the Gigapets or the Spawn toys, so we began taking math expeditions into the toy world. Children set up a chart of various toys and their correlative prices (as determined by small-group consensus). Charts were made. Children were then given amounts of money to spend at our classroom "toy store." Some made choices for themselves. Others made choices for friends and relatives or class members in their working groups. Always, they were required to justify their reasoning and their mathematics. Solutions were shared and discussed. When end-of-year sales ads hit the press, we talked about discounts. "Save 50 Percent," "20 Percent Storewide Clearance" and so on became the content of math workshop. Two dollars off of an item at one store was compared to a 25 percent savings at another. We finished our unit with a discussion of consumerism and the lasting value of toys. We talked about priorities in spending money. All of this was very real for them. Having been allowed the fantasy of shopping with imaginary money, they were able to consider the reality of limited funds.

Another math project that used money was our work in planting native plants in our school yard. Children assisted in the writing of grants. They wrote letters to local businesses to ask for donations and discounts. Children visited nurseries and exchanged their labor for reduced plant prices. Comparisons were made in class discussions between the amount and type of work they performed and the discounts they received.

After being awarded one grant, we divided the children and funds into four groups. Long discussions followed about the type of plants we needed. Each group was given $100 and we went to a local nursery. Children spent two hours touring and considering plants. Each group was determined to get the most for their money. They selected plants, added prices, calculated discounts, and negotiated with each other. In the end, we returned to school with many beautiful plants. After class discussions about the location of individual plants, children planted. Entries in their learning log were full of botany and math! They expressed their feelings and demonstrated their investment in the projects.

Motivation is not an issue when the problems are real for children and math becomes integrated into the classroom culture. Often a child will bring a problem to class or the class will suggest a math problem. Chloe, a fifth grader, recently welcomed a new sister to her family. Mila, Chloe's sister, visited the class soon after. As her mother spoke of birth weight and length, one child hatched the idea that we record this information whenever Mila visited during the year. Out came the graph paper. When graphs were set up, we decided to anticipate Mila's growth by placing a point on the graph every fourth week for the remainder of the year. Children would estimate Mila's growth and compare it to the actual statistics we would receive as she visited.

Listening to children has made me aware of the math that I use at home and school. Very often this math lends itself to classroom problems. As I wonder about water usage at home, miles per gallon in my car, or miles hiked on a weekend, I share this with the class and we investigate the math. Purchasing lumber for a deck became a math exercise for the class. By noticing and discussing these problems, children have become aware of math use by themselves and their families.

Learn Those Facts by Heart

Who knows their times tables by heart? Christine came in one morning and announced that she knew her nines by heart.

"What do you mean?" I asked.

"Just listen," replied Christine and she went on to recite her multiplication facts.

Other children chimed in. "I know my fives by heart."

I asked, "What does this heart stuff mean?"

Children were confused and tried to explain that they knew them without thinking.

"Show me where in your body you know your facts."

Most of them pointed to their head.

"So," I asked, "don't you know them by head?"

This conversation led to the meaning of the term "by heart." We discussed what might be learned by heart. Some children said that you learned friends' names by heart. Others spoke of places that they loved. We talked of learning poetry by heart when we loved the poem. All agreed that learning by heart was not as difficult as learning facts. We decided to change the phrasing for our purposes. We would now call it "learning by head."

It may seem unimportant, but I believe we need to teach children to slow down and be aware of language that we take for granted. Thoughtless assumptions establish categories of "known." We tend to accept these categories without condition. Such acceptance establishes paradigms that cultures have been willing to murder and pillage for. Thoughtless paradigms allow us to mistreat the environment. Teaching the children to attend to language and meaning will keep them alert to other parts of their lives.

Beware of the Lurking Poison Method

As I began to discover the power of children constructing their own thinking in math, I found myself dismayed by adults sharing algorithmic "tricks." In September, I carefully worked with the children to build a math workshop. The environment emphasized meaning and understanding. Children worked at their own level. Discussion was a central part of the process, but children learned not to accept the thinking of others if they didn't understand it.

Then in November, the Thanksgiving holiday brought the relatives. A well-meaning uncle, aunt, or grandparent often asks about school, then proceeds to share the short cuts of algorithms. Proud students returned the following Monday, anxious to share their new adult tricks. We listened to Marie excitedly share her work.

$$\begin{array}{r} 23 \\ \times\,17 \\ \hline 161 \\ 23 \\ \hline 391 \end{array}$$

When I inquired why the lower twenty-three was positioned like that, children assisted Marie by responding with, "That's the way my grandpa learned it" and "My aunt said you have to line up the numbers." It was not grounded in place value. Discussing this situation, our staff began to refer to this as poisoning the children's thinking process or "the poison method." Before long these very words entered our culture. Children would ask us when they might learn the poison method. Or they would complain to parents who were teaching the poison method. This continued and we felt that we had armed these children with a protection against math without understanding. We took time at conferences to explain our position about math construction to parents. Newsletters further explained the idea. One parent wrote back:

> After reading your Newsletter under the heading "Curriculum Talk," I am prompted to reply with my agreement on this topic. In reliving my childhood educational experiences through Marilyn, I compare the two and find that they are not the same (and I am thankful that they aren't). While I was strong in some areas, I was (and still am) very weak in others. This lack of confidence resulted in a fear of certain subjects (mainly mathematics) that has carried me into my higher education. The way in which I was taught to think in school limits a person's view of the world, how things interact, and how we can apply our skills realistically. The world is not compartmentalized into reading, math, and social studies. It only makes sense to teach children that all things relate to each other.
>
> The integration of all subjects of study *is* the way of the future and builds problem-solving skills that extend far beyond the classroom. My father says you can't teach someone common sense (and in some cases I would agree). However, this style of teaching encourages true intellect and that, in turn, results in common sense.
>
> I am very happy with Marilyn's progress and enthusiasm this year. I am also very pleased that her teachers are constantly learning themselves and equally enthusiastic about educating students in a way that will benefit not only the student, but society as a whole.
>
> Sincerely,
> Adele

My teaching was moving along fine until the Andersons entered the program. They received the same talk as everybody. But one January day, Sheila, their third grader, came in excited.

"I learned a new way to multiply."

"What do you mean?" I asked.

"Let me show you." Sheila proceeded to demonstrate the multiplication algorithm for double-digit multipliers.

Dismayed, I asked, "Sheila, why do you write the numbers like that?"

"To get the answer."

"But why are they written in this manner?"

"That's the trick. My father taught me."

I was frustrated. Angry. Undermined. I thought these parents understood and here they had by-passed the process of construction and understanding. We called the father in immediately and explained the situation. He simply said that he had been sitting around with Sheila and wanted to help her with math. We showed him various ways to work with her so that she understood her concepts.

The next year, Sheila was a fourth grader. I sent my newsletter home containing the explanation about math. Sheila's mom wrote this in response:

> Sheila's math strategies (in division) are often so long and cumbersome she makes addition errors in the process and winds up with the wrong answers. We've been working on ways to estimate to use bigger numbers, reducing the number of times she divides in the original number. Can you help her with that? (I'm trying to honor your request even though I personally believe in the immersion process.)

In October, students were solving a problem that required division. Sheila's paper looked liked Figure 3–3.

Curious, I asked her what the "Gees Box" in the bottom corner meant.

"Oh, that's the other way I divide."

"What do you mean?" I asked.

"Well, my mom said I could divide this way at home because it is quicker, but that at school, I should divide your way. So I put both on my paper. I could show you but it's kind of hard."

"Sheila, I know how to work the problems this way. It's how I was taught in school."

Her eyes grew wide. "You do?"

"Sure. I'm just not sure it's the best way for most children to understand division."

I was frustrated. Did these parents not understand how I was teaching? Were they being stubborn? In persisting to teach her the short cuts, they seemed to be undermining the constructivist philosophy. I called Sheila's

WATCH YOUR LANGUAGE · 53

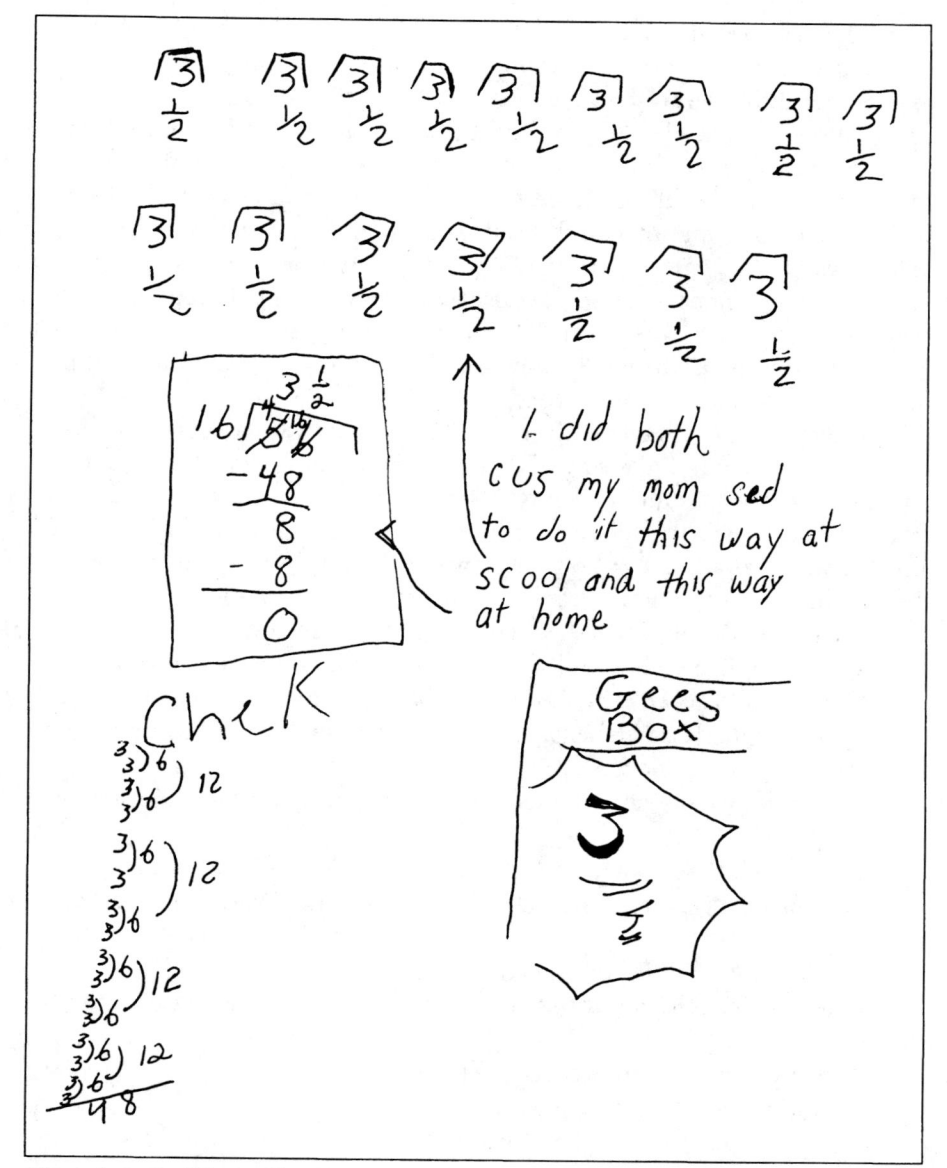

Figure 3–3. *Student Problem Division*

mom in to talk. This time, however, I decided to listen sincerely. I wanted to understand her thinking. When we talked, she explained that she felt there were many ways to solve these problems and that she didn't think it would hurt Sheila to know more than one. I wondered. Sheila seemed confused with her concepts, but pitting teacher against parents wasn't worth the price of pure construction. I talked with Sheila and her mom, requesting that she continue to work in both ways knowing that I would continue to ask her to explain her thinking, strategies, and decisions. Sheila agreed.

This experience led me to reflect on my values and language. Had I tried to create a new tyranny of math process? Had I supplanted one method for another with like fervor? To designate something a "poison method" that had worked for some of us schooled in a previous manner was limiting. What message had I given to the children? Poison is a strong word. In my creative play with language, I hadn't considered the view of children. Poison to them is something sinister from stories about protagonists and antagonists. By saying, "Beware of the poison method," I was saying, "Beware of the adults in your life that seek to poison you."

I had also presumed that they could not hold two processes in their minds at once. Sheila had assumed that I didn't know the algorithms her parents used. Why else would I keep such simple strategies from her? I was perceived to be conspiring to keep children from these secrets. This was just another way that adults kept power from children. In wanting to relinquish the role of gate keeper and create a constructivist environment, I became a new gate keeper of the secret short cuts of math problems.

We gathered as a class and discussed this issue before our winter vacation. This time, however, we talked about the intention of adults. I asked the children if they had had the experience of being taught math computation tricks. Many said they had.

"What do you do when someone begins to show you their short cuts?" I asked.

"I tell them that I don't want them to teach me."

Tory made a gesture of her hand passing over her head. "I just let it do this."

"Yeah. I don't listen," several children chimed in.

Others wondered about them and a few felt they knew these methods already.

"Do you want to know these short cuts?"

Opinions were mixed. Some did and some didn't.

"If you're patient, I believe you will develop them, or at least some very efficient methods of your own. Some of you may discover even better methods."

This satisfied them for the most part.

"But the problem is how you interact with people with respect."

The discussion continued. The class decided that they could listen. Most of them felt that they could ask why certain steps were taken. If the adult could explain it to their understanding, they would learn something new. If the adult became flustered, they would not pursue the questions.

Some decided they would follow Tory's advice and let it go over their heads. We then discussed the idea of sharing their method of solving problems and their math thinking with the adults. Many felt that they would like to try. This could enhance their math understanding because when they articulate concepts, they learn them in more depth without becoming confused.

4
The Continuous Learning Community

Creative thinking occurs in an environment of freedom and diminishes in an environment of oppression.
—ALBERT EINSTEIN

I was in my fourteenth year of teaching when I volunteered to serve on a committee directed to formulate a long-term plan for our school. This task force, including three teachers, one parent, the principal, and a district administrator, attended a three-day planning conference. As so often happens for me, it is the times between workshop sessions that become the important events. I have attended some conferences only to derive more from the car ride with my colleagues than from the actual workshops. This was no exception. Getting these six committee members together in one room was powerfully dynamic. We began talking and spent nine hours each day sharing philosophies, ideas, wishes, and dreams.

We questioned the common practice where children change teachers every year. This is not a reflection of the work place or families. For that matter, we couldn't think of anywhere else in our culture that we change the environment and peer group year after year. We discussed the possibility of teaching a group of children for more than one year, a practice that would allow us to establish a long-term working relationship with the child. Firmly established, this relationship with the child at the beginning of the second year would enhance learning and cut down on acquaintance time. Instead of entering a new classroom, children would get right back to work in the familiar setting after a vacation.

We talked of teacher teams that would be responsible for a child's entire elementary school stay. A team would develop consistent practices and philosophy. The child would know expectations and organization, providing greater time and energy for learning. A small team of teachers working together in a continuous program could greatly enhance the children's success.

As a result of our discussions, two of us were ready to try this experiment. Our principal supported the idea. This was the beginning of a new program. It is now in its seventh year and continues to develop.

The Nuts and Bolts

We called our program the Continuous Learning Community. I had experience teaching children in grades three through six, while Pat's experience had been with special education and first and second grade. Wanting to establish an environment that created the flow between two separate student groupings, we moved our classrooms next door to each other. This physical proximity would reflect our pedagogical consistency. However, it still meant leaving one classroom to enter the other. We wanted the adjacent classrooms to be an extension of each other. We held a class meeting. Caelin thought we should cut a small passageway between the rooms. The class agreed. With the perspective of children, they proceeded to imagine this passageway. The final plan was to cut a small opening in the wall through the coat closet. Luke likened it to the wardrobe in C. S. Lewis' *The Lion, the Witch, and the Wardrobe*. So we cut a passage, large enough to crawl through, between the two rooms. The passage was designed for children. It was two and a half feet by two and a half feet.

As Pat and I planned, we worried about having too large a community. Fifty children in one group was not very intimate. Valuing primary contact with a small group, we searched for a model that would illustrate our ideas. The metaphor we found was family life. We decided that each classroom should be a primary family unit while the other classroom would represent cousins. Cousins visit and sometimes stay for extended periods of time, but then return to their own home. There is joy in the gathering and relief in the departing. This metaphor gave form to our planning.

Next we aligned our schedules so that we would have times each day when all children were involved in the same curricular workshops. This would allow us to share classroom space, materials, and teacher resources. Having been frustrated with fragmentation during the day, we decided to dedicate long blocks of time to our workshops. We divided our week into five primary workshops: reading, art, math, language, and unit study. Workshops were planned as ninety-minute to two-hour blocks. During workshop, rooms were designated with characteristics such as quiet or shared work. Lunch schedules in our school had been established by age: primary and intermediate. We worked with our cafeteria manager and supervision team to adjust our lunch and recess schedules so that children could be together in the cafeteria and on the playground.

Realizing the need for constant revision and refinement, we established three regular meeting times for ourselves in addition to the staff meeting of the larger school. We scheduled one lunch time to discuss individual children, one morning meeting to review our work, and one afternoon planning time. We met with specialists as they developed their schedule so that their work would allow us to work in each other's classroom. At the time, we had a music and physical education specialist who took responsibility for instruction with our class. When my class went to music, I would work in Pat's class.

Staff Development

"What if we don't do anything in math class today?" Pat asked one morning.

"What?" I wondered, still breaking through mental morning fog.

"I wonder what the children would do if we did not initiate anything for math workshop. Aren't you curious to see what would evolve?"

I had taught in four different schools in fifteen years. I liked changes. Starting something new always taught me about myself and my practices. This work, however, had a greater impact than any I had previously known. It was to become very significant to my educational development.

After three years of teaching, I decreased my attendance at educational workshops, conferences, and classes. So many of them offered "revolutionary" new programs and techniques, but they tended to be variations on the same themes. I went through stages of careful workshop selection, leaving early, and nonattendance. By now I was skeptical even to the point of avoiding educational conferences. But my professional growth was about to explode into new areas of experiment, practice, and understanding. The work Pat and I undertook in planning our new program led to the clarification and articulation of our educational philosophy and practice. When we talked about the importance of community activities to begin a day, we asked each other why they were important. We shared and discussed the various ways the same objectives might be accomplished. As I described my dissatisfaction with the increasing fragmentation of the school day and its negative effects on the community, we brainstormed ways to re-create integrity in daily schedules.

My first teaching job had been in a city twenty miles from my home. I rode the city bus to within a half mile of school, then walked the rest of the way. The solitary bus ride and walk to and from school served as my reflective time, time to think about the children and the work we were undertaking. I would review my behavior in the classroom community. I would anticipate and sometimes lament. Throughout that year, I shared my thoughts with other staff members over lunch, before meetings, or after school, but these sharings only touched the surface, while the depth of my reflections were solitary. New ideas were hatched alone. Practices were implemented in many cases without sharing them with another teacher.

In this new program, I suddenly found that my mind was alive. Ideas flowed. Being given control over more of my day freed me to consider and prioritize my schedule. Having a colleague to work in close proximity doubled my creative energy. Creating a new program allowed us to start at ground zero, freeing us to examine our curricular assumptions. Even after school started, Pat and I were meeting for two to four hours per week. We discussed philosophy, plans, children, and our place in the classroom.

Both of us noticed our renewed enthusiasm. I felt myself transitioning from program instructor to educational artist. Having had the experience of responding to many different children and learning experiences during my years of teaching, the philosophy derived from these experiences, and the knowledge of how to create a learning environment, I could enter the room without the baggage of outcome expectations, sequenced lesson plans, textbooks, programs, and worksheets. In their place, I learned to enter with a vision of creativity and excitement about learning possibilities.

Benefiting Children

"You probably should go to the math shelves and get some blocks or something to get started. I'll show you. See, he's going to ask you what you're thinking so it helps to have stuff to point to as you explain. It's okay if you don't know what to do."

It was the third day and I had just started math workshop. Jenny had been in my class for two years and she was explaining things to Michael. Michael was a new fourth grader. Each year, between 40 and 60 percent of the children in my class are veterans. Of the rest, most have been in our program and know me, though they have spent their instruction time in Pat's classroom. There are usually two or three students who are new to the program. This set of circumstances enables a culture to continue from year to year. Older students pass on expectations, schedules, rituals, and routines to younger students. They have established responsibilities like facilitating community sharing and physical education warm-up. Jenny was extending these responsibilities by explaining the setup to Michael.

The members of the classroom community have ownership of their day and year. They anticipate the schedule. They become accustomed to the rhythm of our work. We begin each year with a field trip to a local park where we hike, explore, and play. We end each year with the same field trip. Children plan and organize an overnight field trip around a unit we study each spring. When I make changes in their daily or weekly schedule, I inform them in advance and explain my reasons. If they want to change something in the schedule, they present their reasons to me and we discuss them with the class. In this way, children learn to expect honor and respect. The very structure of every classroom becomes part of the curriculum. As educators, we must build that structure in the same way we develop curriculum.

In math, the culture is very important. Children know that they are to take their work seriously, investigate, question, experiment, explain, share, and learn. They know that they can ask each other for help but that they have the onus of understanding. The teacher and the learner become one team focused on mutual comprehension. Jenny and Michael had become that team for the moment. Through explaining, Jenny was reinforcing her understanding of the math workshop process. Michael was getting individual instruction about it.

One October day of our first year of working together in the Continuous Learning Community, I noticed that some children didn't seem to understand place value fully. I was working with Russell, a third grader who was hesitant when counting large numbers. He had trouble deciding which number in a sequence was greater than another. I met Pat at lunch and we talked about him. She informed me of Russell's personal history in math. This led to a discussion about what we wanted to emphasize in math. We discussed the importance of concept understanding, axioms, theorems, computation, problem solving, and logic. I asked Pat not to bother teaching multiplication facts but to devote a lot of time to basic number concepts. She agreed, relieved not to have to be concerned about pushing children beyond their natural progression of development by teaching multiplication facts too early. She asserted the exception that if certain children wanted to learn these or were being held up by not knowing them, she would teach the facts. It made sense. We realized the pressures we had previously felt to "get children ready" for next year's teacher. Pat no longer needed to worry about how I would treat the children's specific skills, judge her work, or give mixed messages to the children about any lack of skills or previous education. Working together in a continuous program promotes cooperation and collaboration. In turn, these promote the growth of children.

Children have anxiety about placement. When September comes, they know that they will be working in my classroom. They know me, my style, and my expectations, and I know them. Before I began teaching in the Continuous Learning Community, I would spend the first few weeks trying to learn about each child. I observed, tested, and listened in an attempt to come to know twenty-six individuals as quickly as possible. Some children eluded my understanding until January. Now come September we catch up on our news and continue our work. When it is time for math, we simply check in with each other and move on.

Recognizing that each child has many gifts and talents, we want to avoid academic stratification by age or grade. Older children are never the "helpers." Children help each other, but this goes in many directions. Fifth graders have learned to listen to math practices, ideas, and strategies of younger children. This is not out of politeness, but genuine interest. They see the same interest in all the adults in the classroom. We don't model the behavior of listening; we listen. We don't listen in order to show what "good listeners" look like; we listen because we are privileged to hear someone's ideas or approach to a problem. We listen to learn.

Adults live and work in mixed-age communities. When children have the same opportunity, they form mutually beneficial relationships with other children without developing the age prejudice that was prevalent in so many classes I had taught previously. Instead, they come to know the dynamics of work and play differently. They have options. In math, a child will work with one child on the chalkboard, another with pattern blocks, and alone with learning logs. Community learning affords many opportunities.

Parents and Families

Russell was with our program for five years. His family had become part of the community. We had been to his house for field trips. His parents had worked on fund-raising events. They had spent hours in conference with us discussing Russell's work and progress. They worried about him, and taught us to watch a quiet child closely, to attend to coping skills he developed to avoid notice. They approached us at our closing parent night and asked if Jonathan, their one-year-old, would be in our classroom one day. They felt tied to the community and wanted to continue their involvement.

Our district staff have realized that when we are working well with a family, it is important to maintain that relationship. Therefore, providing parents agree, we prioritize our placement so that siblings will be placed with the same teacher an older brother or sister had. Continuing relationships with families, as with children, allows us to focus more on the child.

Pat's job is to inform parents of our philosophy. We have a conference with each family at least twice each year. Since most of our new students are first graders, Pat is responsible for conferences with these families. During the first year, she uses the child's work to explain the philosophy of our program. Commonly, parents end up working math problems using tens blocks and other manipulatives. Pat explains the importance of allowing children to develop their own understanding and processes.

Jim was skeptical of this at first. A father with postgraduate degrees, he was very confident in his math ability. When his daughter, Em, began explaining how she had worked a problem to transform a bar graph into a circle graph, Jim questioned the work. He believed that it couldn't be solved without applying proportion to the equation circumference equals pi times the radius. While his daughter went on sharing other work, Pat invited Jim to keep working on his equation. A few minutes later he exclaimed, "She's right!" Unable to follow her thinking, Jim had taken an alternate route and proved her solution. He was impressed by his daughter's work though he still didn't understand it. He was amazed that she could derive strategies while he had been given formulas to memorize assuming only some distant, great mathematical thinker had derived them. Jim assured us that he would allow Em to create her own processes and listen rather than try to get her to conform to his thinking and process. This attitude of respect for children's work becomes part of our culture. Parents value it and talk with each other about it.

We have had many parents spend time in our classroom. Sometimes they work math problems alone, sometimes they join groups. These participants rejoice in new understandings, replacing their own rote computational strategies. Thus, community becomes a center for learning. Sometimes we talk about our classroom as a recycling center—a place where people can come in and experience steps they have missed in their own learning and education.

Jean, Paul's mom, was totally frightened of math. Her own school experiences had left her without confidence and understanding. In September, she volunteered to work in our class. I suggested that she help with math. "No way!" she replied. She decided to work in writer's workshop. After a month, I approached her about math again. I thought I could learn from her about our math work. Assuring her that she needed only curiosity, she decided to give it a try. I asked her to observe and ask questions in order to learn what children were thinking. When the first workshop ended, she was amazed at children's work and articulation. She expressed a willingness to continue. Over the course of the next several months, Jean began to participate more and more with children, working with small groups as well as individuals. Her sincere curiosity and sensitivity to allowing the children to be in charge were a great benefit to our workshop. Her presence kept children focused, encouraged them to articulate clearly, and precipitated important questions to their investigations. At the end of the year, Jean thanked the class, saying that she received more than she gave. She had been embraced by the community.

We often find students wanting to return to our program. Some come out of community service, others asking for help. After graduating from our program two years earlier, Robin visited to ask if she could work with us on her math. I was surprised because Robin was such a strongly grounded math student. She felt that she needed some review and that Pat and I could help her with algebra. We didn't want to become tutors, but we invited her to join our class and see what she could gain. On her first visit, Robin expressed amazement at the level of algebraic problems some the children were solving. She began to join in their groups and listen to their strategies. Following our instructions, she didn't share the theorems and equations she knew from her seventh grade algebra class with the children. Instead, she worked the problems with the children allowing them to lead. Through this work, she was able to synthesize the concrete process of the children's work with her abstract strategies. Without any direct instruction, she achieved a solid understanding in algebra. The community supported her learning.

A Continuously Evolving Process

The difference between a community and a program is that the former is alive and ever-changing, while the latter is built upon repetition. The variables of the community are the individuals within it. In our case, it is the children and parents. The teachers also become variables as they continue to learn and explore. In this way, our community defies definition. Its specifics grow and change.

We now have four members of our staff. The staff meets each week to discuss what is working and what is not, what to continue and what to discard. We plan in response to the experiences of community members. If Emily is going to visit Disneyland, Ryan's dog had puppies, or Joe spent the weekend with his grandmother, the community responds. This response might be sharing the event with the entire class or connecting two children to share experiences, writing, or formulating math problems.

Likewise our philosophy needs to change in response to the community members. When we first began teaching math together, we were sorting out sequence and scope of concepts and practices. Then we evolved to radical constructivism, defending the need for children to derive everything on their own. Currently, we recognize the need for some students to be guided in strategy derivation. We see the benefit for others to work from an algorithm to its proof. We see math in every subject and every unit we study. Our program and our philosophy will continue to grow as we grow and as we meet new students and parents.

5
Unpolluting Ourselves, Unpolluting Others

The very first tear he made was so deep that I thought it had gone right to my heart. And when he began pulling the skin off, it hurt worse than anything I'd ever felt. The only thing that made me able to bear it was just the pleasure of feeling the stuff peel off... Well, he peeled the beastly stuff right off—just as I thought I'd done it myself the other three times, only they hadn't hurt—and there it was lying on the grass: only so much thicker, and darker, and more knobby looking than the others had been. And there I was as smooth and soft as a peeled switch and smaller than I had been.

—C. S. LEWIS
The Voyage of the Dawn Treader

Trouble was brewing for a fifth grade student in my class. Teachers complained that she was disrespectful and defiant in the halls. She would not allow herself to be directed at recess. Yet somehow, we had found peace in the classroom. Much of the reason was that she felt extraordinary about her work in math. It was, in fact, extraordinary. Robin had never wanted to learn in the same sequence as other children. She checked out books from the library in third grade that were large, cumbersome, and too difficult to read—she didn't care whether I thought she could read them. She wanted to skip the small steps.

Math was the same. Robin's learning was more punctuated than sequential. She wanted to explore all the edges. I proceeded with her through many concepts. My only requirement was that she develop the understanding and strategies herself, then spend significant time mastering these concepts. One day she chose to work with fractions. We created fraction bars out of construction paper, drew pie graphs, used pattern blocks, and played games. Within two weeks, she had a firm understanding of the meaning of various fraction numbers. She could combine them in addition, regroup into equivalent fractions, and solve subtraction problems.

When Robin asked me to explain the multiplication and division of fractions to her I was stuck. Of course, I knew the algorithms: multiply the denominators then the numerators for multiplication, invert, then multiply for division. But why? If I was to assist Robin in building her understanding, I would need to understand the foundation of these concepts myself. To achieve this understanding, I had to divest myself of my knowledge of algorithms.

For a week, Pat and I sat at the table of a local bagel shop at lunch time struggling with the multiplication and division of fractions. We used scores of napkins, filling them with our diagrams and drawings. Moving from the "known" to understanding was not easy. False starts and stalls were marked with our language. Why is the product resulting from the multiplication of whole numbers greater than the multiplier or multiplicand, while with fractions it is less? Intuitively, multiplication causes increase. Working with language we figured that $\frac{1}{2} \times \frac{1}{4}$ worked with the vocabulary of one-half of one-fourth. Realizing that this was "short speak" for $\frac{1}{2}$ of a group of $\frac{1}{4}$, we derived a new understanding of the language and mathematics of fractions.

The traditional algorithm directed us:

$$\frac{1}{2} \times \frac{1}{4} = \frac{1 \times 1}{2 \times 4} = \frac{1}{8}$$

The language-derived method says:

$$\frac{1}{2} \times \frac{1}{4} = \frac{1}{2} \text{ group of } \frac{1}{4}$$

So we start with $\frac{1}{4}$ and designate $\frac{1}{2}$ of that figure (see Figure 5–1).

Given this new language, I was able to work with Robin. We talked and referred to the diagrams. Years of training polluted my thinking whenever I was not watching myself. While working with Robin and talking to her, I had to stop myself, mentally return to the napkins at the bagel shop, and carefully

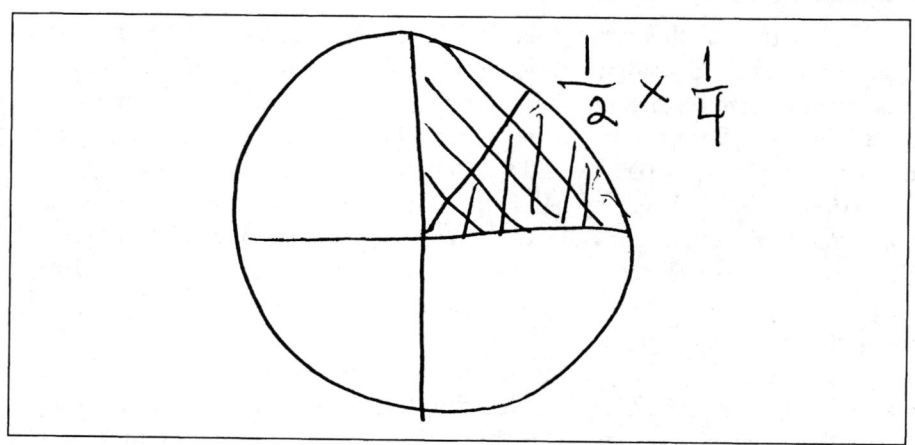

Figure 5–1. *Fraction Graph*

proceed. Three years later, I still find that I need to keep the bagel shop fresh in my mind or I slip back into the language and obscurity of traditional fraction algorithms.

What Do You Want to Be When You Grow Up?

I was in second grade attending a private parochial school. My teacher was Sr. Bernadette. It was a difficult year for me. The homework was long and tedious. Sr. Bernadette ruled the class closely with little leniency and less compassion. Her ideas and values were presented to us as law. I was hit with a ruler for sitting with my foot underneath me. We were kept in all recess because one student was missing an eraser. We memorized the five principles of living things and learned to make a swan out of the number two. Talking was limited to precise answers. Somehow, through this experience, I began to separate myself from the student sitting in my desk. Inwardly, I questioned Sr. Bernadette's rules and her concepts and critiqued her discipline. Outwardly, I appeared as a student who quietly followed rules and avoided her disapproval. It was that year that I believed I could find a better way to teach. It was the first seed of my career choice.

Wanting to teach children with care and compassion led me to this profession. My university training included examples of activities that would motivate children and help them learn. I delighted in the "bells and whistles" approach to teaching. All the while, my vision was to be in front of a classroom full of happy, joyful, engaged children. During subsequent years of my career, I continued with this vision I had created at a young age. Teaching is a very fulfilling profession. The success I experienced with children reinforced my practices. My style consisted of taking concepts and strategies that I had learned in school and passing them on in a positive, enthusiastic, systematic manner.

A fracture in this almost flawless career emerged when I transferred from teaching third grade to middle school. Seeing my class list in August, I was excited to note that many of the children who had been in my third grade class were assigned to my new class. The first week of school consisted of a happy welcoming of new and familiar children to a sixth grade community. After a week, I began to assess the skill level of the students. I was disconcerted to find that many of the children who had been in my third grade class could no longer accurately compute the same algorithms. What happened? They had learned my methods, enjoyed their work, and achieved competency. How could they forget?

That year I began a journey of reflection on my practices, research into learning, and focused observation of children. Questions emerged continuously. What enables children to remember beyond their work in class? I likened much of my previous work to a radioactive isotope. Given a sufficient infusion of energy, certain fundamental elements can be temporarily transformed into other elements creating isotopes; however, the isotope remains unstable. When the energy is withdrawn, the isotope reverts back to its former state. Is this what was happening with the children in my class? Were they able to successfully compute math problems only while I supported their thinking and work? What would happen if I didn't teach them? Did school make a lasting difference?

All of this led to the ultimate question: Who am I as a teacher? What, ultimately, is my role? My choice had been to teach children in an environment that was not oppressive. I wanted to unveil my truths in a joyful manner devoid of fear. I came to this profession out of care and a desire to serve. It was difficult for me to realize that the intention of service is not enough. It was hard to undertake a journey of self-reflection, ego deconstruction, and unpollution.

Freedom from the Known

J. Krishnamurti wrote a book in 1969 titled *Freedom from the Known*. He states that what we know is a major barrier to our ability to learn. When we believe that we know someone we have lost touch with them. In that losing touch, we cannot possibly know them. Could the same be true of our work in math? Certainly, my work with Robin and fractions leads me to believe that when I "know" math concepts, I don't understand them. I often find in working with children that I must interact with the concept, materials, and child as if for the first time in order to be capable of response to the child's thinking. I must free myself from what I know.

A teacher recently called me into her room. She was excited about a huge step a child had made in developing mathematical patterns. Working with patterns of sequential complexity, this child had leapt ahead, skipping two of the anticipated steps to a more complex set. This was done without hesitation, explanation, or the use of intermediate steps. It was surely a gift that had heretofore been unnoticed in this child. As the teacher celebrated this new observation of the child, I couldn't help wondering if the real gift was that she had given the child enough space and time to create his own work. The teacher, due to her programmed thinking, assumed that the children would need to pass through a certain sequence of steps. When this child created his own way of moving through the sets, the teacher felt he was gifted. Often, we judge children as fast, slow, gifted, challenged, competent, or handicapped in reference to our own thinking and the strategies that we know. We are polluted by our assumptions. I wonder how we would be assessed if the standard could be shifted to the child's thinking.

Everything We Do Is Damaging

Pat, my colleague in our elementary program, is a brilliant teacher. She creates math problems weekly that are as outstanding as any I have seen. I often feel that if I followed her around with paper and pencil, I could develop a program from her work. Both of us, however, shudder at the thought of a math program. Programs respond to only part of the important ingredients of math curriculum. The variable that is too often ignored is the child.

We had been involved in discussions about what children create on their own and how we unintentionally direct these creations. One morning, Pat announced that everything we do is damaging to a child's development of their own knowledge. I asked her to explain. She said that she had developed a lesson for her class this morning. As she began to gather the materials, she suddenly realized that she had a plan of how this particular problem would be solved. This is what stopped her. Not only would she betray her expectation of how she thought the problem should be solved, but she was organizing material accordingly. Together these would lead to Pat's imposition of her thinking on the children.

Pat is not one to succumb to self-doubt or deprecation. Our conversation had the atmosphere of new discoveries about ourselves. It was one of amazement and interest. It didn't stop either of us from proceeding with our math workshop for the morning. Rather it gave us a new way of observing our children and ourselves. We began to take more care in the preparation of our math workshop. We tried to find our assumptions that might pollute the children's work.

Education: The Great Experiment

I learned about the combustion engine from my 1962 Chevrolet pickup. I had owned a few cars previously, but the pickup was the first car that was not in proximity to my father's garage. Two hundred fifty miles from home, I scratched my head, scraped my knuckles, asked everybody who would listen, and learned how to keep that vehicle running. I was amazed to discover that car repair was an experiment. Trouble starting my truck in the morning led me to a local gas station. I explained the symptoms and the mechanic advised me to replace the battery cables. If that didn't work, check the battery. The next culprit in line would be the starter. Relieved to have a direction that would end my starting troubles, I went to work. I replaced the battery cables, but it still wouldn't start. I pulled the battery out and carried it in a cardboard box to the gas station to test it. When it tested out in good condition, I knew I had found the culprit. Crawling beneath the truck, I pulled off the starter. Trading it for a rebuilt one, I assumed my troubles were over. However, gloom settled on me when it still didn't work. I revisited the mechanic and was told it must be the solenoid. Replacing the solenoid proved to be the solution to getting my truck running.

That experience taught me that car repair was an inexact science. It was a best-guess experiment. There was no great mystery, just experience gained from trial. The mechanic follows an if-then flow chart. I began to look around at other venerated institutions. Medicine soon became as obviously experimental as auto mechanics. Doctors made a best-guess diagnosis most of the time. Sometimes they would have to follow up with alternate treatment because the original problem persisted. In extreme cases, organs were removed unnecessarily. The art of medicine, as the art of mechanics, meant gathering information, comparing it to previous experience and knowledge, forming a plan, and hoping for the best.

The same is true in teaching. Variables in the automobile or body are complex, like the variables in learning. Similarly to the doctor or mechanic, educators learn to listen and observe. We try a method to teach a child a skill or concept. If that doesn't work, we must have another strategy.

The Grand Unified Theory

Stephen Hawking, like many present and past physicists, hopes to find a Grand Unified Theory. This achievement will allow us to relax, because we will finally understand the workings of the universe. It will mark an end to speculation and a beginning to the taxonomy of physics laws under the hierarchy of the grand theory. It will make things simple. Others say that our own limited capacity renders us unable to conceive of a Grand Unified Theory. These people believe that such absolutes will always be constricted by our present belief systems. Like the discoveries of Ptolemy, proven incorrect in time, cumulative knowledge will change the perspective. The political and social struggle that arises in education is similar to that of physics. It would be simple and tidy if there were a Grand Unified Theory of Education. Teacher education programs could teach it. Teachers would practice it.

Teaching, like medicine and mechanics, is an inexact science. Many of us have tried to follow recipes for teaching. New programs rise with fervent support every few years. There's ITIP, Math Their Way, Multiple Intelligences. . . . The only certainty is that no program will last. Why? Madeline Hunter was a wonderful researcher and theorizer in education. I had read her work since I began teaching. Ten years into my career, I learned of Instructional Theory into Practice, her program based on the principles she had developed. A local district was offering an ITIP workshop, so I signed up. The tenets of Madeline Hunter were presented to us in the first class meeting. They were reasonable and I accepted parts of them. In the second session, however, the practice of these tenets was demonstrated. Teachers, posing as students, were asked to stand in front of the class and told that they would be tested on class material right after its presentation. The idea was that investment in learning material based on the known need to repeat it and the fear of embarrassment would increase the level of retention. It worked, but I was unsettled. Why should we use fear and stress to teach? I left class to give myself time to think. Realizing that I didn't want to teach through anxiety, I disregarded the theory. Still feeling disconcerted, I wrote to Madeline Hunter and questioned the practice. She returned my letter, writing en route to a conference in Japan. The tone of her answer was angry and frustrated. She asserted that her work was not based on the methods I had witnessed and that she could not be responsible for the interpretation and exposition of her work in classes around the country. In fact, her program had been changed to fit the predominant mindset of local teachers. Her ideas were meant to spark observation, reflection, and discovery. Instead they were polluted by local assumptions. How we long for an easy answer. Sometimes we behave as if thinking is a chore instead of a joy.

In recent years, an administrator with incredible vision has been leading teachers away from programmed curriculum, scope, and sequence. In their place, she has worked with staff to develop themselves as mathematicians, scientists, and sociologists. She believes that we teach who we are. But her work has not met with large-scale acceptance. Many teachers lament the loss of textbook adoption, grade level sequencing, and standard curriculum. They are highly critical. What is it that they fear? What is it that they want?

Computers, I am told, have given a great advantage to program teachers. Having lesson plans on a computer enables them to call up the next set of lessons in a sequence, justify the date and pace the sequence. With the touch of a key, they can print out a week's or month's lesson plans. I am not able to work like this and still stay fresh. Since I have begun to be a partner in learning with children, I look forward with anticipation to math class. Each day is new and I can't preplan for a week of math classes. I outline my ideas for children during workshop, but prepare to adapt to their thinking and discoveries.

Too often, teaching is a solo event. Needing to control learning, teachers struggle to get children to focus, work, and recall concepts. Between planning, assessment, school, and district meetings there is little time to reflect, let alone meet and discuss questions and observations with fellow professionals. Yet this, too, is part of our pollution. When we begin to change our focus and shift our priorities, we will create self-directed learners and we will become learners ourselves. I am becoming a student and researcher of math and of education. Math workshop is my opportunity to learn. As this perspective becomes common in our profession, we will be on a constant cycle of hypothesizing, observing, discussing, and evaluating our ideas and practices. Staff meetings will change dramatically. They will become conversations about children and learning. Educational conferences will cease to advertise "lots of activities and handouts." Instead, they will feature considered reflections, supported hypotheses, and discussion.

Tabula Rasa

John Locke proposed his theory of tabula rasa in the seventeenth century. He believed that when children were born their brains were a blank slate. Experiences along the way filled the slate like furniture fills an empty room. A look at our practices and textbooks indicates that we still believe this theory. In addition, many of us often teach as if we believe the slates of the children are homogeneously filled at the beginning of the school year. If all children have the same slate, it makes teaching simpler. "Class, open your workbook and turn to page twenty-six."

We must realize that children are inextricably tied to the accumulation of their experiences. By age five, children have had an enormous amount of experience with math thinking. Even in kindergarten, children's slates are radically different from each other in the area of math. Any attempts to align the level of skill and knowledge of a class are misguided. They force children to behave in ways that are not congruent with their knowledge, skills, and curiosity. They demand conformity over curiosity and construction. The variations in children's experiences challenge us in the creation of classroom community and learning environment, the establishment of relationship, and the selection of strategies from our pallet.

I was visiting with a community of home-schooled children and parents recently when someone said, "James is interested in division. How would you talk to him?" I realized that I would not talk to James about division, but would talk to him about himself, his relationship to math, and why he cared about division. I spent the next forty-five minutes doing just that. James was an interesting child. He was sincere in his interest. I realized, as we talked, that he knew about division.

James' mother watched our work keenly. When our time was gone, she told me that she had read that math should not be taught formally before the age of thirteen. She wanted to hear my response to that. We didn't have time to develop a substantive conversation, but I knew James was a happy child with a strong foundation in language, math, and curiosity. I told his mother that as far as I could tell, whatever she was doing with James was working. Relieved, she responded that she had so much fear of math that she was happy not to teach him this. James was lucky. It made more sense for him to be mathematical in the world without formal training than to experience math mixed with anxiety from his parent.

Many of the children we teach are not as fortunate as James. Teachers and parents are often ashamed because they are afraid of math. Historically, survival needs have encoded human beings to respond dramatically to fear because it was linked with quick learning in survival situations. Children needed to fear swift rivers, poisonous snakes, and predatory animals. Learning needed to be quick and lasting. A toddler who ignored warning could end up tragically hurt. Fear helped ensure survival. It was the tool adults used. Learning to become sensitive to fear in others allowed children to anticipate danger, so they developed the capacity to sense fear in others, particularly adults. Children still sense fear in adults, including teachers. In the classroom, if children receive two simultaneous lessons, math and fear, they will respond to and learn fear. They will link fear and math. This is a fundamental subliminal dynamic. It is a cause of much pollution in our math teaching.

On the other hand, some children are raised on the assumption that "none of us are good in math." This was the case with Grace. At our conference in the fall of her first grade year, Grace was sharing the work she had produced from her learning log. When it came to math her mother said, "I expect math to be a struggle. No one in our family is good with math." We made an effort at every subsequent conference to point out Grace's "good" math work. We tried to encourage her in this subject. By the time she was in fifth grade, Grace was a competent math student, yet she always frowned when it was time for math work. She shied away from math discussion groups, sharing of strategies, and showing her work to me. She had internalized the belief that "none of us are good in math." Fortunately for her, when she went to middle school, she found herself in a math class where the teacher was impressed by her skills and made an issue of it. Her understanding and skills stood out relative to other students. She was moved to a class studying more advanced concepts. Grace came back to report that she was indeed "good" at math.

Our goal for Grace and all students is that their reference point for self-assessment is within themselves. But sometimes environmental conditions pollute this. As in all cases, it is our responsibility as teachers when a pathway is blocked to find alternate routes to learning. In this case, the learning was about herself. The art of teaching requires us to understand the child as well as the content and create a relationship between these two.

I think young children are more open and receptive to learning because they have accumulated fewer concepts and misconceptions. Most of their experiences are new, so they are often engaged in the construction of knowledge. Sometimes stressful situations arise that create impediments to learning. These include misunderstanding of concepts, feelings of inadequacy, confusion, and comparative self-assessment initiating from the home, classroom, or culture. Some sources of learning impediments are subtle, such as the discrepancy of gender role models in mathematic occupations. It is necessary for teachers to develop strategies to respond to such learning blocks, untangle them, and unpollute the child.

Teaching Without Fear

As teachers, we must be clear and confident in our ability to direct children, understand curriculum, and present situations that will stimulate and support learning. When we achieve this, we become artists in the profession of teaching. An obstacle to achieving this goal is the teacher's manual. Full of activities and built on sequence, it tells us when, what, and how to teach. The manual is specific, prescribed, and efficient, but it circumvents our delving into mathematical content and neglects response to children. It allows us to teach math when we don't completely understand it. Such action can lead to immediate and frightened practice and create a formulated, impersonal environment.

At a math workshop a couple of years ago, one of the teachers remarked that she didn't need to learn algebra because she taught only primary grades. She was quite comfortable in her track. She believed that expanding her exploration to algebra might confuse her and even shake her confidence in the basic operations. This teacher needed a lot of time to build her fundamental concepts in math in order to move through these limitations. Even though she was behaving competently as a teacher, following prescribed strategies to lead children to learning, she was not comfortable with her own math. She admitted to near panic when a child in her class wanted to learn more. What a message to give to children! What fear to pollute them with! Until we are given the time and encouragement to be continuous learners, we will hide behind screens of curriculum content and sequence.

6

Don't Hold That Pencil, It Takes Half as Long

When the people know more than they understand, the state will be in deep trouble.

—LAO TZU

In the past decade, it has become important for me to learn computer skills. I attended many workshops. After receiving instructions, I would attempt to apply new concepts and strategies. Sometimes I got "stuck" not knowing what to do next. After asking a the instructors questions, they would explain while their hand grabbed the mouse or punched some keys. This quick sleight of hand left me confused and frustrated. Having too many participants in need of attention, they had developed a practice that seemed efficient. Sometimes, they didn't have the language or thorough understanding to articulate the solution process. Though the computer was "unstuck," I wasn't. It was too fast for me to comprehend. I hadn't shared the problem-solving process or developed skills for working through future problems. Realizing the importance of guiding me in the process to solve my own problem, I formulated a rule in my classroom: Never touch the keyboard or mouse when someone else is sitting in the chair directly in front of the computer. The same axiom applies to holding a child's pencil in math class.

I'm Too Busy Right Now

My classes consist of twenty-five to forty children. Traditionally, I viewed my role as an air traffic controller, monitoring and guiding all of the activities at once. I was proud of my ability to organize material and retain so much immediate information about each child. My years of teaching had helped me develop into an accomplished "juggler" of instruction. I would have children working with many concepts and computations simultaneously. I refined my skills, using them to develop individualized and small-group instruction.

I was very impressed by my work until I met Karen. Hired by our district as assistant superintendent and curriculum director, we soon became colleagues and friends. Karen talked about teaching and shared her classroom experiences. Visiting my classroom, she offered observations and questions about the work we were doing. I soon recognized a common theme in these inquiries. Karen was looking for a depth of understanding demonstrated in work and conversation. I felt frustrated that I didn't have time to develop the depth of thinking considering all the curricular responsibilities I was given. We talked about schedules and time. Karen scheduled her work so that she could spend time regularly in my room to pursue this investigation. That time turned out to be during math learning.

During the preceding five years, I had developed an individualized math program including self-pacing, progress checks, and evaluation. The program was working very well, which, for me, meant that children were receiving high scores on standard assessment and moving up the math sequence ladder. Ignoring the mechanics of this program, Karen would enter the room, sit next to a child or two and work intensely, giving no attention to the rest of the classroom environment. She would spend as much as a half hour with one child, talking and asking questions. By the time workshop had ended, Karen would have talked to three or four children while I had talked to twenty. Yet I was envious. Her talk seemed to have precipitated movement in a child's thinking, while much of my talk had been giving directions, monitoring behavior, recording progress, and ensuring the smooth flow of the individualized program.

Throughout the year, we discussed the differences I noticed in our behavior. Karen always assured me that I could have a successful workshop while intensely interacting with only a few children. However, there was a catch. I had to stop controlling the classroom. She convinced me that my intense work with a few children would positively affect others. Listening to my conversations, they would hear the types of questions I asked and begin to value the discussion of mathematics. Slowly, I started to experiment with this method and found it very rewarding. I felt good about this change in my practice. Children began to demonstrate a new depth of understanding in their math work. As I transformed my behavior, the classroom atmosphere changed to focus on inquiry and investigation. With the end of each session, I had a greater understanding of the mathematical thinking of children. The shift in my teaching took a couple of years of experiment, self-monitoring, and adjustment. It continues today.

Whose Lesson Is It?

I often have people working with me in class. Stressing the need to listen to children and allow them to find their own way through problems, I still notice the difficulty adults have allowing children the freedom to be in charge of their work.

After working with a child one morning, I stood and saw Laura lying on her side on the carpet. I watched as her adult helper had Laura's log and pencil. Laura, meanwhile, was looking anything but interested. Her eyes wandered toward the ceiling while this helper scribbled on the notebook and talked. Laura had lost power over her work and her interest waned. Later, I asked this adult how it went. The response was that Laura had gotten off track but had been set straight. All was well now. Had this lesson been a success? A setback? It was a very clear math learning experience for the assistant. She had understood where and how Laura became stuck and successfully figured a way out. It also became a success when I pointed out what I had noticed regarding Laura's involvement in the solution. I shared my axiom: Never hold the pencil, it takes half as long. It is a metaphor for allowing the child to take control. We discussed the importance of giving the child the luxury of time to accomplish learning. We discussed the benefit of frustration and the supportive role of conversation.

What about Laura? Was it a disaster for her? No. Laura had seen someone listen to her, care about her thinking, successfully understand her process, and be motivated enough to solve the problem. Fortunately, Laura gets to work through her own problems most of the time. One of her strengths is that she has learned to be comfortable with ambiguity—an imperative to any student of mathematics. This comfort or lack thereof drives math classes and guides teachers. I find when I am not comfortable with a process I tend to want to hide this from students or adults. Before I realize it, I am moving through the place of uncertainty at a brisk clip. I behave as though a quick solution will shade my doubt and confusion. Though such action is justifiable and helps preserve an ego, it is not the best way to teach. It serves the teacher, not the learner.

Let Children Think for Themselves

Eratosthenes was a Greek mathematician credited with proving that the earth was round and measuring its circumference and diameter. His experimentation and observation simply involved putting sticks in the ground and watching their shadows. He noticed that stick shadows varied with times of day. Longest shadows were formed at dawn and dusk. He then compared shadows of sticks in his city of Alexandria to those in a neighboring city, Aswan, at the same time of day. These shadows were different lengths. Through this work, he was able to break out of the paradigm of thinking the earth was flat. He could solve the shadow dilemma by creating a model of a spherical earth. Applying the geometric principles of Euclid, he drew models in which he extended the lines of sticks and shadows. In this extrapolation, he estimated the diameter of the earth with remarkable accuracy. Further applying this geometry to the curve and distance between Alexandria and Aswan, he predicted the circumference of the earth.

The ontology of our knowledge in astronomy is rife with examples of people who freed their thinking from the dominant world view. Mostly, they were driven by a need to justify their observations and make sense out of them. Our understanding of the universe is incomplete. Astrophysicists such as Stephen Hawking are still trying to integrate observations and mathematical principles.

Does our work in public education enhance the ability of children to choose sense and reason over rules and paradigms? Do we hinder extrapolative thinking of this nature? Are our practices opening thinking or controlling it? Galileo was forced, by religious leaders, to discredit his findings regarding the heliocentric solar system and spent his last years under house arrest. I have known teachers to lower the grades of students who solve problems in their own way rather than the standard algorithm—their own form of house arrest.

Colleen came to visit from the middle school. She was excited to talk to me about math. Having been "promoted" recently from foundations to pre-algebra, she felt proud.

She exclaimed, "Today we learned how to divide decimals."

"Congratulations. Tell me what you learned."

"Well," she replied, "you move the decimal point of the number you are using to divide to the right however many spaces it takes. You move it until there are no more numbers."

"I see. Do you understand why?" I asked.

"Yeah. My teacher said that if you move it to the left, you make the decimal longer and you don't want to do that. You have to change it into a whole number."

"What next?"

"Then you take the number you are dividing into and you move that decimal the same amount. You can add zeros if you have to. Then, if you need to, you add zeros to the answer."

Even with some of her language unclear, I had no doubt that Colleen could successfully compute decimals using this algorithm. I didn't press her for understanding but allowed her to feel proud. Still I felt sad that such a brilliant child who had developed strategies and practices and demonstrated incredible promise and clarity in thinking was learning the path of following the rules without understanding. When we demonstrate strategies and solutions, we are holding the child's pencil. We take away possibilities of alternate strategies. We separate the child from the process. I only hoped that someday Colleen would remember how to break away from the established rules and strategies so that she might serve us with great discoveries in medicine, astronomy, math, or any number of fields in which she is capable.

The Art of Standing Back

I lived in a small community complex while attending college. The grounds were frequently visited by skunks searching for food dropped by residents. A friend and I enjoyed watching the behavior of these animals and we discovered that skunks do not spray immediately when threatened or scared. One morning we saw a skunk approached from the rear by a dog. Hearing the potential danger, the skunk raised itself up on four toes, raising its tail as well. Standing in place, it bounded around in a three hundred sixty–degree circle. As it did, it looked for the danger before choosing to deploy its dreaded weapon. In this case, its warning was sufficient and the dog left. Thus the skunk was able to conserve its own energy and the dignity of the intruder.

Teachers could learn much from the wisdom of the skunk. A fundamental premise of Karen's work with me was to wait and observe before acting. As I learned to focus my work with one or two individuals, I often became aware of the rising noise level in my room. Karen would always ask, "What is the noise? What are children talking about?" Like the skunk, I learned to raise my head and alert my senses. Almost always, I heard children talking to each other about their math in meaningful ways. I learned to stand back from the class and let them develop their math work through their conversations.

Similarly, watching two or more children discussing problems and strategies, I sometimes become anxious at the direction of the talk. It seems to be leading away from the process that I have in mind. I worry that misguided methodology will be employed and entrained; however, children usually figure this out without interference from me. They can see when they are off track and will ask for help if they need it. Most often, they like the power of solving it for themselves. This will accompany them through life as they encounter problems.

"My birthday is in fifteen weeks. How many days is that?" Ben asked our primary class one morning. The group decided to figure it out. Math logs were retrieved, tens blocks brought to the rug and children quickly settled into their work spaces. Tom found his place on the carpet working alone with his log. He had written the problem:

$$\begin{array}{r}7\\ \times 15\\ \hline\end{array} \quad \text{and then rewritten it} \quad \begin{array}{r}15\\ 7\end{array}$$

Tom had not worked with algorithms in multiplication but did know repeated addition. The work on his paper looked suspiciously like a borrowed strategy. Pat's impulse was to redirect him with a statement such as, "Tom, you work multiplication problems with tens blocks. Go get those." Resisting this, she took a breath and watched. Slowly, Tom began building a familiar pattern:

DON'T HOLD THAT PENCIL, IT TAKES HALF AS LONG · 79

```
 15   15   30   45   60   75
x 7    7    6    5    4    3
```

Counting on his fingers, he was moving to a new level of abstraction while synthesizing our work with t-charts and multiplication.

If Pat had not caught herself, hesitated, and watched, Tom would not have had a chance to elevate his thinking and skills to this level. So often, we interfere with children's work. In my class I have children who are identified with learning disabilities. These children are targeted by adult specialists who work in the classroom. With all children, I emphasize thinking for oneself and formulating questions. One morning, I presented a group of students with a problem that I thought was simple. I told them that I was not interested in their solution as much as their ability to show in numbers, diagrams, and words, their process. Soon after they began their work, a resource specialist entered the room and approached a student. After a brief question, the child responded by physically turning her back and saying she wanted to work this out alone. The adult recognized the importance of honoring her need. Looking a little sheepish, she left to work with another child. Later, she came back to the first child and initiated a conversation. I came to their workplace and asked how everything was going. The adult immediately began to tell me how this child was solving the problem. I stopped her and asked that the child be allowed to explain. Later, I explained my reasons. Regardless of accuracy, this student had demonstrated some important skills and needs. The ability to know and express her needs, the desire to work independently, and the confidence to tell an adult that she wanted to do so were significant steps to independent learning. She happened to have solved the problem correctly in a very unconventional way that may not work every time, but she had further developed her ability to create strategies.

The Payoff of Patience

During independent reading time, children are involved in their own books. I circulate through the classroom, taking turns reading and holding a conference with them. One such time, I came to Nat, who was deep in thought.

"Nat, can we read together now?"

Nat looked up at me, startled. "Can you come back to me? I'm having a big idea."

Quietly I moved away. Nat was on an individualized education plan for language processing and math. He had trouble relating to other children in class and was unable to get work completed on time. Nat was often involved in "big ideas." At times, I was frustrated because I couldn't participate in his mental process. His ability to articulate did not match his ability to cogitate. But I learned to give Nat a lot of time for these ideas and usually it paid off. On this particular day, he was struggling with a concept that consumed a lot of his thought and time that year. It was understanding Einstein's theories of matter and energy. In the spring, we studied biographies. Nat chose to read about Albert Einstein. His presentation to the class was very much like a professor's lecture. He filled the chalkboard with diagrams and formulas, clearly explaining a good portion of Einstein's work. He was able to gear it to the understanding of some class members. It was only with ample time and control of his own work that Nat could have accomplished this. He taught me to be patient.

There is a story about a child and a butterfly. Finding a chrysalis, the child removed it from a tree and held it like a treasure. It was a marvel; a miracle ready to happen. Carrying it home, he eagerly showed it to his mother. She counseled him to set it on the windowsill and watch it over the days, but leave it to its own time. The child however, could not wait. Finally, giving into desire, he began to blow warm air on the chrysalis. It started to move. Excited, the boy continued and to his delight the chrysalis opened. Out came a butterfly. The boy clapped and danced with delight. Shortly, however, the boy saw that the butterfly was not developed completely. It's wings were crumpled and small. After struggling for a while it died and the boy grieved.

Like the butterfly, ideas develop in their own time. The transformation comes through the child's constructive process. Without care, I can be impatient with a child who is forming a new concept. My first response will be to grab the pencil or chalk and demonstrate. This is quick, simple, and neat, but it forces the idea too soon. Learning to watch and wait, however, I see children constructing their own concepts. I used to fear that a child would fall behind, but now I realize that the emerging idea will be beautiful and powerful. Not only will it serve a particular math problem, but it will become a blueprint for the child to construct ideas and solve problems. The process allows the child the confidence and mental constructs to think independently. Sacrificing short-term efficiency has a large payoff in the long run. It is like driving a car. When I am a passenger in a car, I talk, look out the window, think, and daydream. Rarely do I pay attention to how I am getting where I am going. Later, I get in the car to drive someplace I have been numerous times only to find out that I am uncertain of the way. When I drive, I learn the way. In the classroom, I want to put children in the driver's seat. When trust in process is established in the culture of the class, children know and work with it. Independent construction of knowledge is an expectation of their work together. They learn to allow each other to work through problems. Often children in my class will say, "Don't worry Tim, I'm not telling him how to do it, I'm just helping him straighten out his thinking."

Jessica visited from the middle school recently to show me her grades. This seems like a fall ritual for children who have left our program. Grades are a new experience for them. Jessica was especially proud of her math.

"I'm so glad you made us explain our thinking. I understand how to work the problems and talk about my work. Other kids can't do that so I'm suddenly really good in math. When I was in your class I wanted to strangle Momo, but now I am glad for every Momo problem we did."

What I aim for as a teacher is not just the ability to solve problems, but the ability to be a problem solver. My goal is for children to feel confident, competent, and have the skills to think through the problem.

The Practice of Homework

There are different schools of thought about homework. It often provides the review and practice of patterns and concepts that class time does not permit. Children learn a pattern, axiom, or rule of an operation in school and complete exercises at home to ingrain it. This work is tedious for the student and difficult for a teacher to review. Teachers, therefore, spot-check a few of the problems or have children correct the work in class. This thinking follows the idea that any new skill, be it basketball lay-ups, juggling, or riding a bike, must be repeated to be learned completely. This makes a lot of sense and follows our observations about learning. I believe it has a couple of pitfalls. Imagine learning to ride a bike and being asked to spend forty-five minutes every day spinning your feet in circles in the bicycle kick without going anywhere. The motivation of riding would soon be lost. Who wouldn't get bored practicing the subskills over and over again? The reward of learning to ride a bike is incorporating the skills into activities that do more than just develop the skill. They allow the learner to experience the joy of riding. The beginner can feel wind in her hair or a sting in his eyes. Math algorithms are just this; subskills of the activities of math. We must discover the activities of math that create enjoyment, and thereby generate motivation.

Additionally, the child must first have built the strategies for solving a problem. Since this is strictly an individual achievement, assigning the group a large number of problems risks having some students work beyond their skill of understanding. Such practice can lead to learning an approach that is not accurate or one that is not grounded in understanding. At the same time, we risk requiring others to needlessly practice previously mastered skills.

Sometimes homework is used to introduce new concepts. Teachers ask children to try to understand a concept that has not yet been taught. Allowing the child to feel ambiguity and confusion first, then "enlightening" them with standard algorithmic procedures will generate the "aha!" or "I get it now" from students. In theory, this works for the child while giving the teacher the role of magician or holder of truths. Some children I have observed, however, decide not to invest themselves in the work of knowing, but wait for the teacher to tell them. Since they correct their own papers while the teacher explains, they don't choose to delve into the problems. Other children become confused and convinced that they are not capable math learners. They relegate math thinking to teachers.

Another homework practice is the challenging mind puzzle. Some teachers call these horizontal extensions. They are math puzzles aimed to develop mathematical reasoning. My family has spent evenings around the dining room table working on these. It has proven to be a fun family activity though sometimes frustrating for the child who has the assignment. Occasionally my children at home work on these extensions independently. I always hope that the teacher gives plenty of time for discussion of the problem, explanation of different strategies, and support for children whose families are unavailable to help or unable to work on these problems.

I carefully consider homework. My goal is to reinforce the integration of math into the lives of children. I will ask a child to teach a strategy or game they have learned to a family member. Their assignment is to report to me about the experience. Children are asked to share new skills, create math problems, or notice math in their home. Homework is aimed at extending authenticity and meaning.

The Practice of Timed Tests

Fourteen years ago, I was hired to teach third grade. I worked with another third grade teacher. Our place, in the math sequence, was clearly delineated through tradition and articulated by the fourth grade teachers. By the end of third grade, children were to know their math facts and be able to compute in all four operations. I inherited traditional methodology including sheets of math facts divided by operation and number of problems on each sheet. The plan was to time children on these facts regularly. They could feel their success as they progressed through these sheets with more and more problems in the given allotment of time. Multiplication sheets started with twenty-four problems and incrementally grew to one hundred problems per sheet. Cleverly, I developed a system of individual pacing and record-keeping. Children were given five minutes to finish a sheet. When they completed a sheet with at least ninety-five percent accuracy, they were passed to the next level. I would celebrate their successes. Anyone who completed all of their tests joined me in an evening pizza party.

This system lent itself to clear record-keeping and tracking of children. My expectations were evident. I could talk easily to parents demonstrating progress and comparing a child to class norms and target expectations. Graphs were created to share at conferences. The crack in the wall began when I observed children no longer reading problems on tests they had taken numerous times. Instead, they were recording memorized rows of correct answers. I ignored this, thinking that on the next sheet, they would have to read and answer individual problems. More striking to me was that some children simply couldn't pass the "tests" and actually seemed to lose competency. Conferring with them, I heard descriptions of racing hearts and sweating palms. Regardless of my attitude of fun and belief in their ability to succeed, pressure was limiting them.

I began to wonder about my practice. I saw how unauthentic my methods were. I questioned what price was being paid for these skills and what hidden curriculum was occurring. I wondered if there were other ways to approach this work. We discussed the dilemma as a class. The reaction was split. About half of the children wanted to continue the process and half wanted to end it. I asked them how they learned their facts. Many different methods were reported from repeated written work to playing games at home. One thing was clear. All children who felt successful participated in activities directed toward learning facts at home with adults. Children without this support didn't have the power to create it. They were working in a void. It was another case in our society where school practices reinforce and maintain socioeconomic stratification. We ended up with an optional self-correcting timed test and a variety of class activities to learn facts. More importantly, we were able to reduce the level of anxiety for children in class. In time, I dropped the practice entirely.

Recently I talked to a high-school teacher. I asked her what she wanted from teachers of elementary school in math. Her answer was quick and pointed, "Whatever you do, don't time their math work. Don't let them equate competency with speed." She was struggling to get her students to create reasonable answers and thoughtful problem solving. The training children had received regarding speed was hard to change.

The Fallacy of Getting Ready

It is difficult to interpret our personal experience as students and parents from within our educational philosophy and practices. Sometimes the experience builds the philosophy without due consideration. When my son was eight, he entered the class of a well-meaning, caring, and very efficient teacher. This person spent uncounted hours during evenings and weekends correcting, recording, and responding to children. Still, my son was losing his confidence and skills in math. He had a half hour of math homework every night. After a few evenings of tears about class, I scheduled a meeting with his teacher. I described his frustration and lack of confidence. I also expressed how much I missed playing games with him in the evening. She responded with a story of her son. He had done well enough in school, including high school. But when he went to college, he was shocked and overwhelmed by the amount of responsibility and homework. Consequently, he dropped out. Based on this experience, she made a decision to assign homework so that they would be prepared for their future. The present struggle would pay off in college. She didn't realize that this practice might create immediate resistance to math. To her credit, after lengthy discussion, she agreed to personalize her work with my son.

Preparing children for the future is our directive. How we go about that is our dilemma. Do we prepare children for pain and suffering by giving them pain and suffering? By nurturing and protecting them? With adequate skills, will they succeed in future classes? Without skills, will they fail? The variables involved in success and failure are complex. As I watch children, I am as amazed at those who are willing to learn and ask questions as by those who are afraid despite their obvious ability. I can take full credit for neither. But I have concluded that I want children to expect to succeed. I want them to expect to be treated fairly. Combined with my belief that modeling is the dominant tool of learning for young children, I do not want to make their lives miserable. Rather, I want to nurture curiosity and trust. To this end, I oppose the *getting ready* philosophy. In class, we talk often about the next steps in their education. Children role-play how to advocate for themselves and how to ask others to advocate for them. They consider ways to ask for permission to hold their own pencil, formulate their own strategies, and control their learning. In addition, I try to open dialogue with the teachers of older children so that we understand each other and better understand children.

7
Talking It Out

What if children are going astray? Talk to them. Bring them back to solid ground and construct from their scaffold. Ask questions. Help them make connections. Unravel and rewind.

—PAT SCALO

Three Discussions in Three Days

It was Wednesday morning, time for math workshop. Pat and I had decided to ask children in each of our groups the same question and listen to their language as they shared ideas. It was spring, so the children had had many previous opportunities to discuss math. I expected to pose a problem, stand back, and observe children's language. I wrote $15\overline{)45}$ on the chalkboard.

"I want you to discuss something this morning. We've talked about the language of this problem. Tell me how you read and begin figuring this problem."

Adam was the first to answer. "Forty-five divided into fifteen equal groups. I'd start by making fifteen circles, then begin dividing up the forty-five into those circles."

Others agreed.

Chloe said, "I'd just divide it. You know, how many fifteens in forty-five."

The class demonstrated their comfort with the problem. I decided to move to the next level. I wanted to challenge the group. "Okay. That makes sense. Try it with this problem." I wrote $\frac{1}{2}\overline{)100}$ on the chalkboard.

Claire started, "One hundred into one half equals fifty."

Corey continued, "One half fits into one hundred two times."

Twenty-six children were sitting in a circle on the rug. Discussion was slow. They were thinking carefully. Their words were shadows of ideas that formulated in their minds. The discussion wasn't directed anywhere in particular.

Veronica asked, "How many times would you have to have one half to equal one hundred? That would be two hundred?"

Ryan stated, "Two halves of one hundred is one hundred."

I continued to sit and listen. I wondered if the apparent chaos of randomly shared thoughts would turn into dialogue. Would they begin to respond to each other and build on others' ideas?

Catlin was the first. "I get it using Corey's idea, but my answer is different. One fits into one hundred one hundred times so one half must fit into it two hundred times."

Eve ventured, "This is a strange problem because one half is less than one."

Following Eve's thought, Ofer asked, "Isn't it that if you divide something you should be lowering the number, not increasing it?"

Chloe answered, "Yes, but is it the same in fractions? If you multiply, it's different because they're so small."

Shaeny tried to apply her method of computation. "If I made a circle you could put the whole hundred in it. If I made a half circle, couldn't I put the whole hundred in it? I think so."

Eve picked up on an earlier idea. "What I don't get about Catlin's theory is you can get one into one hundred one hundred times. I don't think that's the question."

Veronica tried to clarify. "It means *what* times one half equals one hundred."

Eve's reply surprised me. "That really makes sense."

Looking bewildered, Ryan said, "This seems an impossible problem."

Catlin got to her feet and went to the chalkboard. "Look. I can show you." She wrote the following on the board:

100	equals
4	25
2	50
1	100

"Look at the pattern. Each time the number we divide into one hundred gets smaller, the answer gets bigger so one half would be two hundred."

"I get it," said Chloe. "We are breaking it into one half instead of dividing by one half. It's like half a dollar."

Eve replied, "But that's divided by two. . . ."

I was delighted with the discussion. Children were engaged and responding to each other. Their ideas seemed to emerge from the thinking of others. They continued for another fifteen minutes and then broke into small groups to discuss and solve the problem.

The day before, Pat had posed the same question to her class. These children were younger; first, second, and third grade. At a parent conference that afternoon, I was able to hear a recount of their discussion from Ed, a second grader.

"We had trouble at first. Most of us thought the answer would be fifty, but some weren't sure. Agneshka said, 'I do know how many halves are in one hundred. One fits into one hundred one hundred times. One half fits into one hundred two hundred times.' It made sense, but didn't she change the problem a little bit?"

Two weeks later, Pat and I were at a math symposium. We were leading a workshop with teachers about language and math. I decided to pose the same question. I asked participants to form small groups and discuss the problem one hundred divided by one half. I asked them to search for the meaning of this problem. As we walked around the room, we heard many interesting questions and statements:

"Yes, but when we come up with fifty, we are breaking it in half instead of dividing by one half."

"Well, a dollar divided in half is fifty cents or half a dollar."

"Yes, but that's divided by two."

"If we change the one half to 0.5 then we know that 100 x 0.5 = 50."

"If you divide by a smaller number, you get a larger number."

"How many groups of one half are in one hundred?" "Two hundred." "Right. How many halves are in one hundred?"

"Let's think of how many halves we have to take out of one hundred. That's an easier problem."

What an equalizer math discussions can be! Similar language and inquiry developed in all three groups. The teachers asked the same questions as the children. Our knowledge of algorithms is based on memorized rules that work for us as long as we recognize an algorithmic category and remember to employ those rules correctly. Adult teachers are able to successfully demonstrate proficiency with the use of these rules. We can teach others the rules and their application. When it comes to understanding the language and concepts of these rules, the minds of inquisitive children are as strong as our years of experience and teaching. Children are as capable as we are of discussing and understanding.

Math Workshop: Finding a Place to Talk

A great deal of talk needs to accompany math if understanding is our goal. Math, after all, is a form of communication. It exists to express ideas within and between members of society. It becomes part of the language of our lives. In consideration of teaching, math talk takes place between children, adults, and children and adults.

Math workshop is a structure that is built for talk. In a two-hour block, it has the time to incorporate class discussion, mini lesson, individual work, collaboration, and personal instruction. I build this workshop into my schedule for a minimum of two days each week. One day is designed for the investigation of number relationships and one for the application and development of strategies in problem solving. During both of these days, there is time for individual project work. On days without workshop, I have a short twenty-minute period for math exercises. This is a time for computation of one- or two-number problems. I reserve Wednesday and Friday mornings for math workshop. On Monday and Thursday, just before lunch, we undertake math exercises.

Math investigation begins with a discussion. This might be based on a question such as, How big is infinity? I might ask them to discuss their strategies for solving given equations. After discussion, I share my workshop plan. Usually, this includes a combination of study groups and individual work. Study groups are small and focused around a given concept. I have held a session on building an understanding of fractions. We used paper, seeds, and fruit to create fraction pieces while talking about the relationship of each piece to each other and to the whole. Sometimes, children ask for a study group. These requests may come out of the academic goals that they choose. Often children are curious about a concept they have seen older siblings work with such as decimals and fractions. Occasionally, a few students may want to investigate concepts like infinity, negative numbers, or zero.

I try to keep this work free of boundaries. I spend about a half hour with a study group, then leave them to continue together or alone. The rest of my time in this workshop is spent observing, listening to, interacting with, and asking questions of children. It is the core of my math curriculum. This is time to respond to children individually. In response, I can direct my talk with children based on what they are thinking. During these conversations, I might find stumbling blocks, articulation, vocabulary clarification, or concept development that I need to address with the whole group. I pull out ideas and skills that need to be articulated, expanded, or celebrated. On one of these occasions, I noticed that Adam had developed an efficient method of multiplying and taught it to others. At the end of workshop, we shared this with the class and named it Adam's Tree.

Children in Conversation

"I can show you how to do that easier," Ryan said to Marilyn.
"Thanks. I kind of know but I forgot."
I watched as Ryan and Marilyn approached the chalkboard. Ryan wrote the problem.

$$\begin{array}{r} 34 \\ \times\ 23 \\ \hline \end{array}$$

Marilyn had been working on this problem by adding a stack of thirty-four twenty-threes.

23
23
23
23
23
23
23
23
23
23
23
23
23
.
.
.

"Break it into smaller, easier groups first," Ryan instructed.
"What do you mean?"
"Pick a small number of twenty-threes that's easy to add."
"Okay. Five."
Marilyn added five.

```
  23
  23
  23
  23
+ 23
─────
 115
```

Ryan continued, "Now record it like this."

```
   34
 X 23
─────
 115 (5)
```

"Now do five more."
Marilyn began to write again, then stopped. "I already know this. It's one hundred and fifteen."
"Right. So record it."
Marilyn wrote another set under the multiplication problem.

$$
\begin{array}{r}
34 \\
\times\, 23 \\
\hline
115\ (5) \\
115\ (5)
\end{array}
$$

Ryan was using the scaffolding of Marilyn's thinking of repeated addition to build the concept of repeated *sets* of addition in the multiplication of large numbers. At the same time, he was choosing language to explain a strategy to Marilyn, thus building upon his own language skills while reinforcing his concept.

Meanwhile, Ofer was trying to understand decimals. Laura had investigated decimals earlier using Unifix cubes encoded with equivalent decimal and fraction numbers relative to a standard length. Laura was explaining and demonstrating the equivalence between

$$
\begin{array}{cc}
3\tfrac{1}{2} & 3.5 \\
+\,4\tfrac{1}{4} \quad \text{and} & +\,4.25 \\
\hline
\end{array}
$$

In another part of the room, Sami and Catlin were drawing circle graphs to add mixed numbers. While this was happening, Rick and Marco were continuing a discussion from recess regarding a movie one of them had seen. While not every conversation in the classroom was oriented to math tasks, most were. These conversations reflected the talk and work I had previously undertaken with individuals. It was evidence of modeling. The workshop discussions included explanation, clarification, and investigation. It demonstrates how children can talk to each other without imposing their thinking and strategies on one another. Each time children engage in authentic math conversation, they add structural support to their own thinking. These supports are neurolinguistic patterns in their brains. They promote physiological change. I think of them as thought highways. Children will be able to access them when the need arises. Additionally, children are building support as a learning community. They develop a network of others to engage in study. A child may talk to Laura about fractions, Ofer about negative numbers, Marilyn about multiplication, and Marissa about division. They are learning how to be involved in the dynamics of a group. All of these are important considerations in a child's mathematical development and social community.

One morning, I noticed that Laura was working with large equations. Surprised, I watched her work. Her problem developed as follows:

```
    257         257         257
  X 125       X 125       X 125
  -----       -----       -----
   1285        1285        1285
                514         514
                          + 257
                          -----
```

"Laura," I asked, "this looks like a new strategy for you. Tell me about it."

Laura turned red. "Well, I had a slumber party with Catlin and Maddie." (Maddie had been in class last year.) I wanted to know what kinds of problems she was doing at the middle school. So I asked her and she showed me this way."

"It sounds more like a math party than a slumber party."

"Yeah, it was. She showed us how to do these, but she also taught us what they mean."

I was elated. What more can I ask but that children are curious about their work, take initiative, and seek meaning?

Math conversations between children develop throughout the year. With each new group of students, I set up a similar math workshop. Often, talk disintegrates into chaos during the first few meetings. I have learned to raise my head above the din and get a sense of the content of conversations. When too many are not about math, I call the group back together and redirect. If I notice some children authentically engaged in math, I will ask them to describe their work and their conversation to the class and then we begin again.

Years ago, as a new teacher, I applied for a job in a small school district. I was asked to teach a math lesson to a fifth grade class in the presence of the school principal and a few school board members. When the class was over, we had a discussion. I was asked if I was comfortable with the noise level in the room. It hadn't seemed noisy to me at all, but it made me think about groups and noise. I began to listen for noise everywhere. I listened in restaurants, libraries, stores, and classrooms. I watched the kinds of activities associated with noise. There was discussion, individual research, introduction, and socialization. I realized that I wanted to build a learning environment that incorporated all of these elements.

My classroom geography extends into the hallway and includes the library. Several times throughout the year, the class examines noise level. They discuss their ability to work effectively within the noise of the classroom. Together, we select areas for conversation and reserve areas for quiet. Within the workshop, they monitor themselves. Students remind each other and the whole class about the place for and volume of noise.

Talking with Parents

"I don't know what to do. When I try to work with her on math, she covers her ears."

It was a parent/teacher/child conference. Alli was an unusual child. She was very intuitive, thoughtful, and deeply committed to keeping her world of childhood imaginings and freshness integrated with the demands of growing up. She insisted upon understanding new concepts before accepting them or even relaxing. She was not satisfied to let a lesson pass without comprehension.

I asked Chris what she wanted from her work with her daughter.

"Well, there are some math skills that I think she needs before entering middle school."

"We have a year and a few months before that transition. Do you want to formulate a plan and timeline for skill work?"

"Yes, but I also want to interact with her about her school work and her day."

I turned to Alli. "What do you think?"

"I just don't get it. She starts telling me what to do on a problem, but I don't know why. I'm afraid of getting confused."

For most of the rest of our conference, we talked about ways they might interact positively at home. Alli offered suggestions. She wanted to share her school-day experiences as they came up. Moreover, she wanted to play board games with her mom, rather than work. School work, for Alli, was tiring. Attending all day was difficult. By the time she came home, she wanted to relax. Noting this and her mom's concerns regarding math, we brainstormed skills Alli would need in the middle school. Together, we created a rough sequence of skills and agreed to meet every other month to check progress. Alli and her mom agreed to spend most of their evening time playing.

I have taught hundreds of children in my career. Each year, I revise my program based on my cumulative experience, understanding, and knowledge about teaching math and the members of the class. I apply new methods. I experiment. Teaching strategies that don't meet with success are discarded. Strategies that I am tired of are abandoned. I have the luxury of years of teaching to refine my practices and philosophy. Yet, each parent has only one or a few children. Parents want to be assured of their children's success each year. They feel responsible for providing their children with the best experience possible.

My teaching is most effective when I am working with the child and his or her parent. We enter what sociologist Peter Berger called a "gemeinschft." It is the structural strength of the triangle combined with the synergetic strength of interaction. The learning gemeinschft between teacher, parent, and child in which all three participate actively is very powerful. It is a most effective partnership. My work is directed by the examination of my practices and the importance of developing a gemeinschft with the parent and child. As I implement new, untried practices, I am cautious and thoughtful. I keep channels of communication open with parents. Usually, the only experience they have in math education stems from their own days in the classroom. They know what worked and what didn't work for them as children. In the ensuing years, they haven't learned about progress in math education. It is my responsibility to inform them of the structure and rationale of my program. This is attempted in several ways. I send a newsletter home each week. One component of this newsletter is the curriculum corner. I articulate some practice and the educational philosophy behind it. Three to four times each year, we gather both classes in our learning community for an evening parent night. The purpose of this night is to demonstrate and celebrate children's work. We incorporate music, literature, math, and unit studies in the presentation without "rehearsal." It is the same sharing children undertake regularly in the classrooms. They may read stories involving math problems or play math games with their parents. For homework, a child might be instructed to teach parents a new problem-solving strategy they have created or discovered. Finally, during parent/teacher/child conferences throughout the five years of our program, we share and discuss practices and rationale.

On our third meeting during the school year, Alli and her mother were more relaxed. Chris was comfortable with the skills Alli had developed. They had begun, tentatively, through games to address math at home. Their play with board games had opened the door for talk about strategies. Chris was delighted by the mathematical thinking and processes that Alli shared. It was with delight that we continued to watch her progress over the next year.

Of Teachers, Workshops, and Staff Development

Several years ago, staff members in our district were called together quarterly for grade-level meetings. While I enjoyed the social interaction of these, I was disturbed by the content. The meetings centered around curricular areas. I remember sitting at one of these meetings while teachers from the host school shared their math work to date. They had "successfully covered" multiplication, division, geometry, and equivalent fractions and it was only Thanksgiving! I left with questions about my teaching. Was I serving the children by focusing our work on process? Was it the right choice to slow down and work with math concepts thoroughly? Would students from my class be lagging next year in sixth grade? This reflection reinforced my value that children understand each concept rather than "cover" it.

Years later, I was attending one of several district-sponsored workshops for elementary-school teachers. The subject was chemistry. One of the things I hoped to learn from the class was the diagrammed structure of the silica molecule. Pat and I had read an article describing a similarity between the structure of this molecule and patterns developed in ancient Mayan art. Before class we had inquired about this, but were asked to wait. During the introduction, the instructor made many fascinating observations. He mentioned the arrangement of elements on the periodic table determined by atomic weight. This weight is calculated using the number of neutrons and protons. It seems, however, that this weight is a bit relative. Not all carbon atoms have the same amount of neutrons and electrons. There are simply a cluster of atoms and most of them have the atomic weight of twelve. It is the mode of carbon weight. I was astounded. Something I had learned to be absolute was relative! Something I had come to know in my chemistry classes as packaged neatly in boxes is a continuum! The periodic table is an agreed-upon representation and classification. I wanted to verify and understand this. Eagerly, I raised my hand to interrupt. After listening to my question, the instructor made it quite clear that we were not here to discuss such issues and that he would appreciate it if I wouldn't interrupt with such questions. I slipped into silence as he proceeded to demonstrate activities we could use to teach chemistry, including atomic weight, to elementary-aged children.

I wonder why our work together is not about investigation, but about activities. While I recognize the value of sharing activities, programs, and lessons, it wasn't until I began actually investigating content and celebrating thinking that my own math teaching began to deepen. The teaching experience of those present at that workshop led me to believe that they could easily create activities if they understood chemistry. Dialogue and investigation aimed at understanding would expand our thinking. It would enable us to create activities and work from a place of understanding.

Mike is a fifth grade teacher at our school. He enjoys stirring things up, tipping complacency off balance, creating cognitive dissonance, and making us think. As Pat and I were beginning our discourse and inquiry into math, he walked into the room one day. Our children were eating lunch in the cafeteria.

"Can you help me out? I have this equation that I want to solve." Saying this, Mike wrote on the board $\frac{1}{2}x + 26y = 42$ and walked out smiling. We took the problem to lunch with us. We plugged numbers in, isolated variables, strained to remember our algebra, talked, and played. Realizing the interdependence of x and y we decided to gather samples of solutions and graph them. We were still working when lunch ended so we left our calculations on the chalkboard. Children were curious and delighted to see us work. We had created a data system or t-chart of solutions. It was a system they recognized from their work. The chalkboard looked like Figure 7–1.

$$\frac{1}{2}x + 26y = 4$$

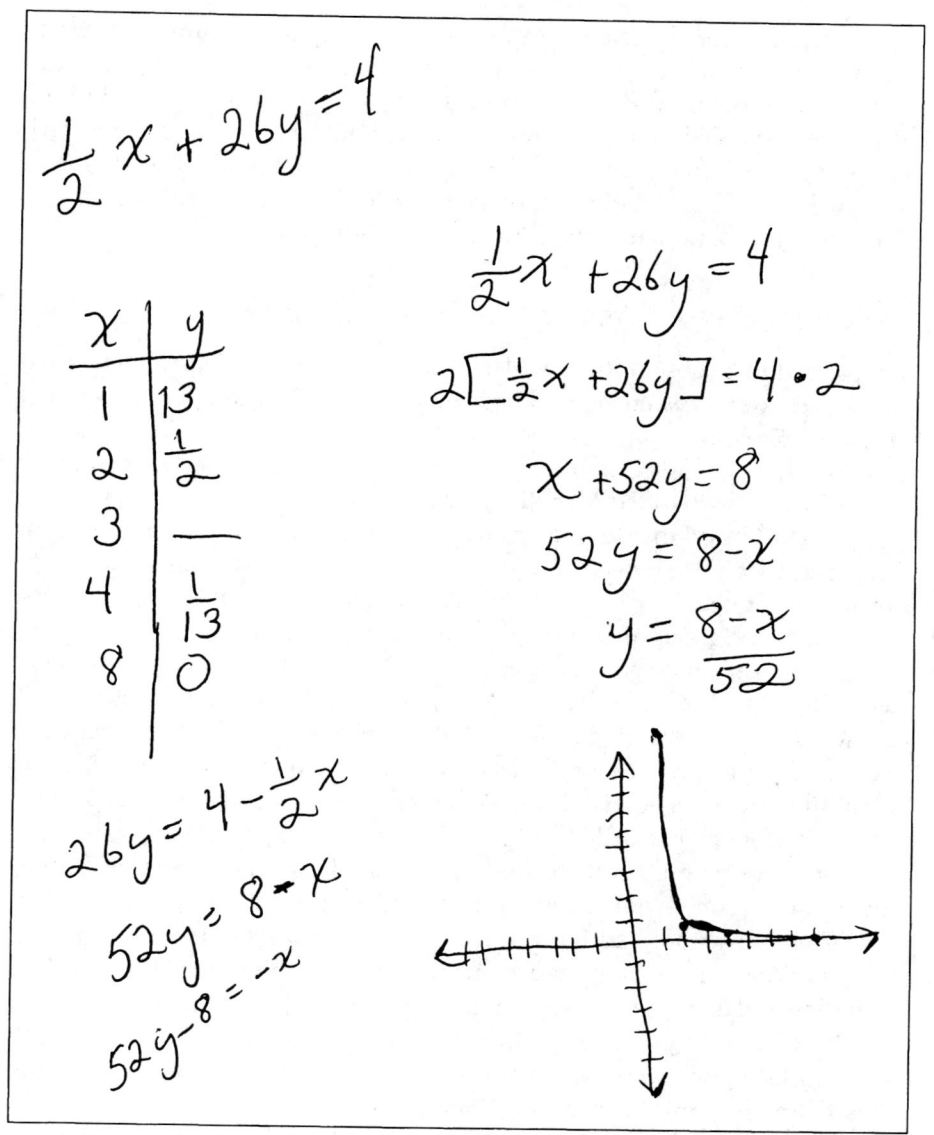

x	y
1	13
2	$\frac{1}{2}$
3	—
4	$\frac{1}{13}$
8	0

$$\frac{1}{2}x + 26y = 4$$
$$2[\tfrac{1}{2}x + 26y] = 4 \cdot 2$$
$$x + 52y = 8$$
$$52y = 8 - x$$
$$y = \frac{8-x}{52}$$

$$26y = 4 - \tfrac{1}{2}x$$
$$52y = 8 - x$$
$$52y - 8 = -x$$

Figure 7–1. *Algebra Problem*

We had collaborated, experimented, made errors, and felt very satisfied. The experience benefited us in two ways. It honed our math skills while giving us the kind of challenging experience we ask of children. Children in our class regularly work on equations that create feelings of capability, frustration, confusion, pride, or accomplishment.

Over the next couple of years, our staff undertook a number of workshops organized around teachers working with math. We solved open-ended math problems, talked about our process, thinking, strategies, and solutions. It was very energizing. We naturally began sharing stories about our experiences with children within the context of this work. The sharing was valuable and authentic. This is the model of staff development that I feel is most useful. It helps me as a mathematician and as an educator.

Talking to Myself Again: Self-Talk and Math

I happened to be absent the day Merrill came to school and shared information about the voices inside his head. He told my substitute that he couldn't stop the voices so he had jumped in a puddle and put his head under water to make them go away. Concerned, the substitute told the school counselor and principal, who called Merrill's parents.

When I heard the story the next day, I was excited. Merrill was a student with special-education needs. In first grade his language was unintelligible to anyone except his teacher, Pat. Merrill had been completely directed by others. Pat and I talked about his lack of inner voice. He responded directly to experiences, but didn't anticipate. He did not weigh pros and cons when making a decision. We had worked to develop Merrill's voice by asking him to tell us what he should undertake during activities. Pat would often ask him to tell her what she would say to him. We had also left him to his own devices for extended periods of time while we observed. I asked Merrill to describe what he heard inside his head before he jumped in the puddle. "Singin" was his reply. Through the ensuing conversation, I realized that Merrill had heard his own voice singing our classroom songs with his peers. He had never heard this voice before.

Children without an inner voice have difficulty retaining intermediate computations, sequencing, and strategies. But all children will benefit by extending and developing their inner voice. Corey didn't enter our class until March of her fifth grade year. On her second day, I asked the class to end math workshop with a response in their math log. I forgot about Corey until I heard Tory explain the meaning of a response to her.

"Just write down what you were working on during math. Give details. Then tell what you were thinking about as you worked."

I ask children to explain their thinking often. I want them to be aware of decisions they make about how to proceed on a problem. It is a skill that develops with time. When they have constructed this metacognitive ability, they can solve problems. Becoming stuck, they can articulate possible solution strategies and evaluate the choices. Metacognition and articulation will serve them throughout life.

8
Of Algorithms, Algebra, and Content

The Dali Lama is a spiritual leader caught up in political events. Exiled from Tibet, he inhabits the border just inside of India and has spent the last several decades supporting the spiritual and physical life of his people. Forced into the political arena to rally international assistance, he straddles religion and politics. A few years back, his travels brought him to southern California. Agreeing to a rare public appearance, he was asked by a woman in the audience, "What is the quickest way to enlightenment?" The Dali Lama bowed his head and cried.

The three R's. Basic Skills. Extrapolative thinking. The debate over content has lasted as long as I have been teaching. With state legislatures getting involved, it promises to continue. How do we balance content and process? What content shall we use as we partner with children in math? What is fundamental and what is supportive?

In reading, the story underlies the skills. It gives purpose to the skills. We don't expect children to grow into adulthood and read the same stories they read in elementary school. Instead, the books and stories create the purpose for the development of skills that will serve the child in the future. The skills will be applied to new content. Adult literacy is evident in the reading of newspapers, memos, directions, and forms. Do we have a similar situation in math? The skills, and the opportunity to use the skills, are the core of math curriculum. What does functional, adult math look like? Does math curriculum dovetail with the math of our culture? When we find the place where content and process merge, we have found authentic math.

The Use and Misuse of Algorithms

Merlin came to visit halfway through his sixth grade year. As always, he was positive. He liked school well enough. When I asked about math, though, he made a face.

"What? You liked math."
"Not anymore."
"What happened?"

"All we ever do is algorithms."

Merlin was stuck on the carousel of skill mastery. He was practicing the quickest way to solutions but he had no passion or investment in the work. I liken it to teaching jump rope skills without the jump rope. One would practice circular hand movements and rhythmic jumping while told that someday we will need these skills. All the while the jump rope sits locked in the closet. In math, children are told they will need skills when they matriculate to the next level in the prescribed sequence. It is true, they may need these skills someday. Yet that someday seems elusive to the student who is promised it throughout schooling. Devoid of application, algorithm practice becomes tedious and meaningless. Meaning comes in the form of application. When we reduce the skills it takes to read, we develop a set of subskills that a reader applies to the content. But they are simply keys to unlock the door of meaning in text. I am frustrated by reading programs that deny books and stories to children until they demonstrate mastery with subskills. They deny children the right to move forward carried by self-motivation. Math skills are similar. The earlier that we introduce meaningful activities to develop, apply, and reinforce the skills, the greater the opportunity for the child to incorporate them into constructed math scaffolding.

The word *algorithm* derives from al-Kworismi, the name of an Arab mathematician of the ninth century. This mathematician constructed many algebraic theorems. In Arabic, the word *algorithm* evolved to mean numerical computation. Later, it included the operations of mathematics and a set of common rules for computation. Herein lies the dilemma for math teachers. We want children to compute solutions to equations. Computation takes a long time if the child must invent a strategy in every instance. A common procedure is efficient. But whose procedure should that be? I prefer to consider the original meaning of the word *algorithm*. I think of it as the individual's constructed set of strategies to solve a type of math problem. With guidance and patience, children will continue to develop the efficiency of their own algorithm.

If we take a look at the operation of multiplication, sequences of algorithmic development might be those shown in Figure 8–1.

Both work, as will many others. A meaningful choice will be made according to the process evolved by the child.

A Time for Every Purpose Under Heaven

I was cross-country skiing. The day before had been sunny, melting the top layer of snow, then freezing it at night. I waited for the day to warm up so that the snow would soften. By eleven o'clock, I was still skiing on frozen snow. I skied about five miles relishing the alone, silent time. But the condi-

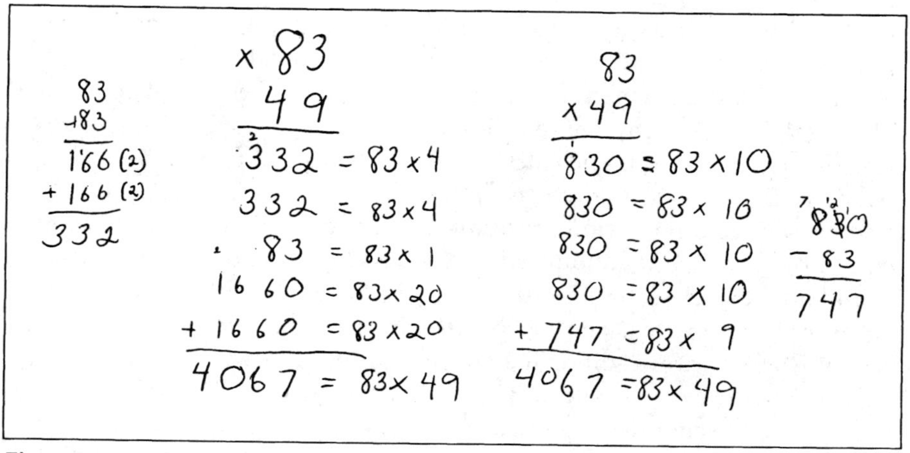

```
      83          x 83              83
     x83           49              x 49
     ───          ───              ────
    166 (2)     ³3̇32 = 83×4        830 = 83×10        ⁷'¹'
   +166 (2)      332 = 83×4        830 = 83×10       8̷3̷0̷
   ──────         83 = 83× 1       830 = 83×10      - 83
    332         1660 = 83×20      +747 = 83× 9      ────
              +1660 = 83×20       ────               747
              ──────              4067 = 83×49
               4067 = 83×49
```

Figure 8–1. *Multiplication Problem*

tions were difficult. Even with metal-edged skis, I was constantly sliding downhill. Grace was replaced with trudging. By the time I ate lunch, snow was blowing horizontally. I realized I should start back. Heading back was not as easy as I had reckoned. Having climbed up a couple of ridges, the usual joy of heading downhill to the trailhead was replaced with the treachery of uncontrolled speed on icy snow. Quick runs left me breathless. I fell many times. My shoulders ached. My quadriceps complained. With a mile and a half to go, I found myself cautiously following someone else's tracks to the trailhead. These tracks were dusted with a half inch of new snow and my skis felt stable. I wondered at my thankfulness to have tracks to follow when I usually disdain another's tracks and search for trackless snow.

Algorithms are tracks in the snow. They are proven pathways that provide a quick way to solution. There are occasions when children can benefit by comparing their algorithmic strategies to others. They may embrace or disregard standard algorithms. They may feel relieved to have the choice to follow one. Each is a particular expression of someone's developed methodology. Some will fit their need, others won't. Our directive is to provide children with the opportunity and autonomy to choose. Besides making choices to incorporate or replace tactics, children see the variety of approaches to math. They learn the similes and metaphors of computation.

Carol longed for a different style of teaching than I offered. She would get frustrated and ask, "Can't you just tell me? Why do I always have to think?" Her mother was skeptical of our program. Perhaps because of Carol's frustration and attitude, she didn't seem to be constructing meaningful, efficient work. During winter vacation of her fourth grade year, she visited her father out of state. When she came back, she was adamant. Her father couldn't understand what math work we were doing and she had been unable to explain. "Just teach me to multiply and divide!" Carol demanded. We talked. First, I listened to her needs and wants. Then I explained why I like to teach meaning and have children construct knowledge. I agreed to try teaching Carol some simple rules as long as she agreed to practice daily and be respectful of other children's constructive development. For the rest of the year we worked on traditional multiplication and division algorithms. At the end of the year, Carol announced that she was moving to a nearby city and would not be in class for her fifth grade year. When she did visit late the next fall, Carol was excited. She felt competent in math. Everyone at her new school worked with traditional algorithms. She fit in with her peer group. Learning traditional algorithms proved to be very beneficial for her.

If I had been unwilling to listen to her and adjust my work, she would have had a difficult transition. There is a time to allow children to construct their thinking, a time to suggest new strategies, and a time to teach algorithms. This is the art of teaching.

Teaching and Training

I consider my work with Carol to be training more than teaching. Etymological examination of the word *train* shows that it derived in the sixteenth century from the term used by botanists to describe how they directed the growth of a plant. Literally, it meant to pull. Sometimes teachers still refer to this derivation in saying, "It's like pulling teeth with this child." I had pulled Carol through the memorization of traditional algorithmic rules and sequences. The theoretical structure was mine. I directed the work, the drills, and the practice.

Training occurs regularly in school. Children become entrained biologically to the school schedule, particularly around lunch and recess. They become hungry at regular times. Training occurs in regard to classroom procedures and expectations. Children learn through repeated practice, reminders, and consequences. In math, training often occurs with such work as memorizing multiplication tables. Mathematical problem solving requires more than training. The child must be able to reason and apply a variety of skills. Training falls short and can even inhibit this work as individuals try to apply strategies without thinking. For problem solving, we must teach children to find and apply their own constructed scaffolds.

The Calculated Dance

Algorithms are tools. They come with training but no instruction manual. They are guaranteed to perform accurately provided the specific conditions are met. They must be applied in the correct circumstance and prescribed steps must be taken in sequence. The same is true for calculators. Given correct application they are a powerful and helpful tool. Knowledge of this correct use is critical. As an adult, I make a situational decision on whether to use them or not. Factors contributing to this decision include the size of the calculation and the availability of the calculator. It would not be efficient for me to retrieve a calculator out of a backpack to see if I have enough cash to buy two or three items at the store. It is quicker to add the prices mentally. I need to know what strategy is applicable. Most often, I use estimation. For small numbers I calculate mentally. These allow me to make most of my decisions unencumbered by the calculator. When balancing a checkbook or justifying a credit bill, it makes sense to use a calculator. The number and length of equations direct the choice.

In class, calculators provide back-up support. Children use them as one method of checking their computations. They don't substitute for personal computation. Children check their accuracy. When there is a discrepancy, they learn to question both their calculations and the calculator. Often the difference results from a mispunched key. They learn to use the calculator for information but not as an authority. Their confidence builds as they feel secure enough to question the calculator. Sometimes our discussion and workshop are developed around the choice of using a calculator, estimation, or personal calculation. Having the skills for all three and the discernment of which to apply frees them to create their own balanced dance of mathematics.

A Place for Algebra

The Arab mathematician al-Kworismi, for whom "algorithm" was named, also wrote a book titled *Algebar wal Muquabalah*. Translated this means *on restitution and adjustment*. Algebra names a system of computation in which symbols represent numbers in an equation. Simple algebraic equations are:

$$3x = 12 \qquad x + y = 4 \qquad 4x + 1 = 9 \qquad 34 - n = 22$$

Though there are specific rules to follow, basic algebra is different only in presentation, not computation of problems in arithmetic. In elementary classrooms, we represent missing variables with a box, line, or blank space.

$$\begin{array}{cccc} 3 & 34 & 8 & \\ \times\ \square & -\ \square & +\ 7 & 6 + \square = 10 \\ \hline 12 & 22 & \square & \end{array}$$

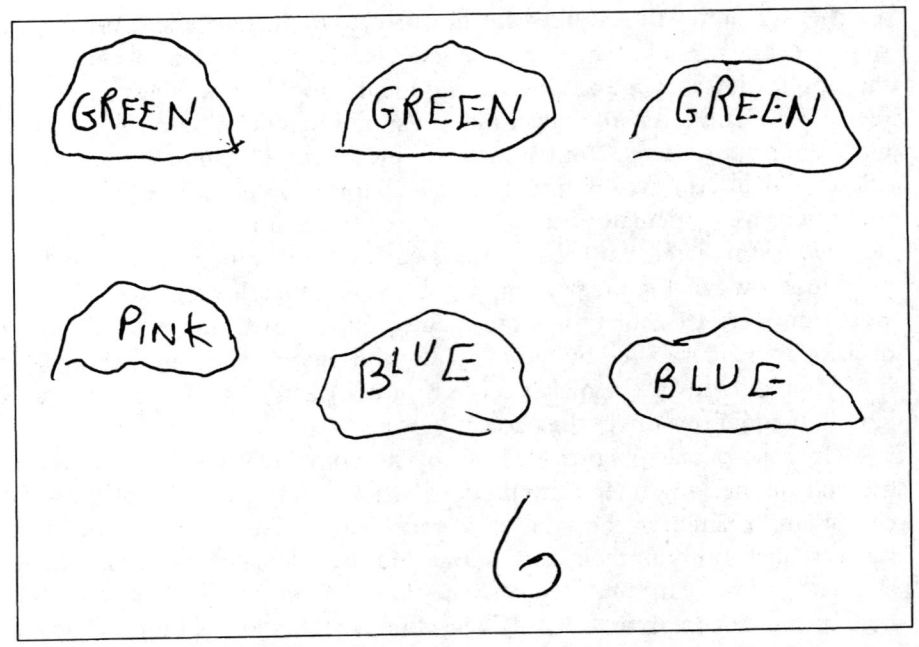

Figure 8–2. Sorting Drawing-Rocks

Sometimes we use algebra in questions: What can I add to twenty-six to make thirty? Five times some number equals twenty-five. I consider algebra to be another way to pose a mathematical question, the way poetry and prose are different ways to express a literary idea.

When we shift the content of our work from computational skills to application, we are shifting into algebra. Simple questions are single variable equations. For example:

> Momo brought a collection of rocks. There were three green, one pink, and two blue rocks. How many rocks all together?

This requires one mathematical operation to solve. Algebraically this question would be represented by $3 + 1 + 2 = n$, but natural symbols of childhood at this stage of sophistication would probably be drawings of rocks as shown in Figure 8–2.

It is the drawings that will become more efficient and symbolic if we let the children develop their own strategies. The introduction of letter symbols to replace drawings at an early stage are too abstract and result in confusion.

Once familiar with the language of these questions, children can progress to problems that have additional variables. Traditionally, these were found in the math extensions section of textbooks and programs. They were augmentations of basic programs, often suggested for "gifted" students. However, these are the types of mathematical problems we encounter in our culture. Placement of application problems within basic curriculum is necessary to develop a mathematical understanding that gives children the skills they need outside the classroom. We must stop teaching math because children need to know a concept next year or because they'll use it someday. Instead, we must extract math questions from their life experiences. We can send Momo to the store with fifteen dollars and offer a menu of purchase choices. Children not only have to solve an equation such that $a + b + c = 15$, but they have to justify their purchases. We can set up questions about the cost of video rentals, kinds of pets, or cafeteria food options. We can ask children to work problems that have more than one answer.

> Mimi has ten cousins. More of these cousins are boys than girls. What possible combinations of cousins can Mimi have?

$$x + y = 10 \text{ and } x > y$$

As adults, a great deal of the math that we encounter has multiple variables. This is true of children also. As they learn to make decisions, they benefit by having the skills to consider more than one solution at a time. They build confidence as they realize that their justification is correlated to the correctness of their answer.

Math as a Component

One spring, we decided to study birds. Outside of our classroom, we have a good habitat that attracts a variety of birds. As we began to plan our unit, we talked about the curricular possibilities of a bird study. In math, we decided to focus on different quantifications of birds. During the study, children walked around school and counted species and occurrences within species. They recorded their findings, developing beautiful graphs that compared times of day, types of birds, and habitats. They used comparative mathematical language to describe birds according to size. They talked about life span, number of eggs, wing span, and migration.

Eli wanted to make a pie graph to record different species of birds he had seen. He started with a bar graph. Pat asked him to recreate the bar graph with unifix cubes. Together, they reformed the cube bar graph into a single line while discussing the correlation between graphs. He rounded the line into a circle and created a circle graph. The process made sense to him. He saw the relationship between the graphs and discovered a process for creating the pie graph. Other students noticed his work, and soon pie graphs were developed throughout the class. Toward the end of the unit, the walls were covered with data presentations, mathematical representations, and art intermixed.

When math is a component, the content of the unit directs the content of math. It provides reason and motivation for the math work. Later we decided to study cats. Pat was reading *Ramona, Age 8* to the class. Picky-Picky was Romona's cat. Pat challenged the classes with the following problem:

> Picky-Picky had 6 female kittens. Each kitten grew up to have 6 kittens. How many cats in all?

We presented this problem to all of the students in grades one through five. Mary Rose, a third grader, solved as shown in Figure 8–3.

This problem led to the notion of exponential population growth and the ethics of spaying and neutering pets. Their concrete and visual work directed the questions of pet populations. These types of exercises led not only to integration within children's math work but between curricular areas.

A Place for Assessment

There are many ways to assess the work and progress of children. Teachers use observation, standardized tests, scoring guides, a national assessment, checklists, and more. I spend the maximum time teaching and minimum testing. Standards keep us aware of norm-based progress, but the most important assessment occurs in the observation and work of a single child. I have never had a class where all children were equal in knowledge, skills, and ability, nor would I want one. Partnering with children means becoming aware of them individually. The assessment tool is keen observation while the recording is anecdotal. Therefore, I keep a notebook with a section for each child. I write during or after class about my work with that child, recording observations, challenges, barriers, and breakthroughs. It provides a quick, clear reference for individual work the next time we meet.

Children record math work in spiral notebooks called "logs." These are a wonderful resource for assessing growth for and with the child. Conferences often consist of reviewing logs and celebrating growth. Parents enjoy flipping through the logs tracking the children's growth and present level of skills. When we have math exercises, children choose the problems they want to compute. I note which problems a child is choosing, the efficiency of the strategy, and accuracy of the solution. If I observe a child attempting problems that are frustrating or too simple, I question the reasons for their choice. Sometimes they have important information to give me about themselves when they describe their choices. Sami once told

OF ALGORITHMS, ALGEBRA, AND CONTENT · 105

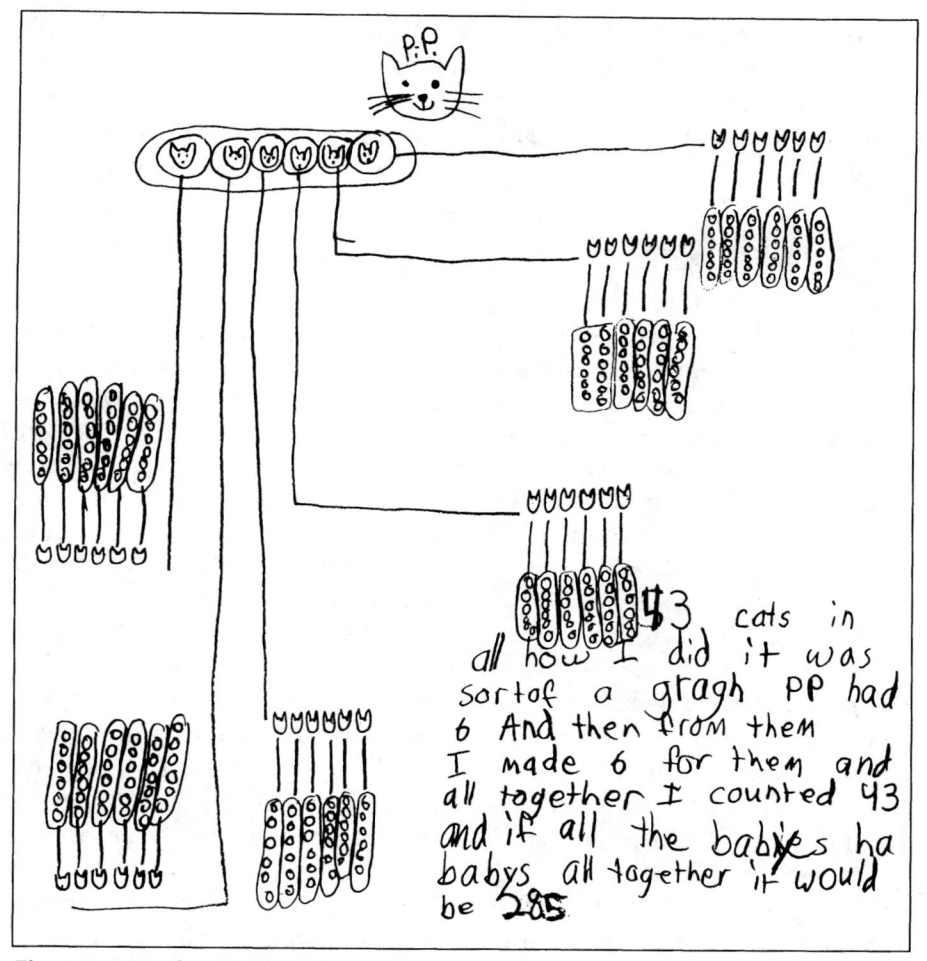

> 43 cats in all how I did it was sort of a gragh PP had 6 And then from them I made 6 for them and all together I counted 43 and if all the babies ha babys all together it would be 285

Figure 8–3. *Student Problem-Cats*

me that she was taking a break from harder problems just so she could relax and review how easy and quickly she solved the simpler ones. She was pacing her work.

    Assessment is important. It informs me about my work with a child, a child's development in math, and my practices. My use of assessment tools must benefit my work or they are not worth class time. Sometimes I am required to give standardized tests. These compare populations of students to each other. I check to see how the class in general compares with state and national norms, but I don't redirect my teaching practices to affect these scores. The norms are too far removed from the individuals I teach. Math curriculum is not about tests, scope, and sequence. It is about creating relationships among ourselves, the child, and mathematical concepts. Understanding this frees me from feeling responsible to "cover" textbooks, compare children, and hold rigid standards. It refocuses me to teaching the child.

A Place for Serendipity

It was June, and we were studying measurement. Precipitated by the fact that we had to move out of our room because new tile would be laid during summer, we were investigating how workers determine how much tile is needed. Offshoots from this investigation led to questions of which room was larger? How many tiles are on the ceiling? What is a square foot? Children were spread throughout the room with meter sticks, measuring tape, unifix cubes, or other material they chose. Some were in the hall, others in the restroom. I was on the floor talking to Max about area. Out of the corner of my eye, I saw an unfamiliar shoe pass. There was an adult in the room. I looked up in time to see a member of our district staff walking across the room pushing a wheel and handle. He lifted it, checked something on it, and left the room. I was on my feet as fast as possible. In the hall, I called to him and explained that we were measuring the room and wondered if he could come in and explain why he was measuring and how his tool worked. He was delighted. We called the class together as he explained how he had measured the room to determine how much tile to order. His measuring device fascinated the children and redirected some of their thinking about area.

Opportunities to halt all proceedings and participate in the unplanned events at hand are a very important part of our content. They demonstrate the reason for math work and they lead to new investigations. Events may include spotting a flock of birds outside a window and estimating their number, comparing attendance in different classes in the peak of flu season, or graphing how many times the computer crashes in a month. An atmosphere of collaboration and investigation between teachers and students is created by linking the classroom with other life experiences. We want investigation to infuse the classroom environment.

Inside, Near, and Far: A Curriculum Model

During my first three years in education, I studied curriculum development and leadership. I observed classrooms, critiqued texts, and studied the curriculum models of Zais, Tyler, Eichhorn, and others. I hung these models on a bulletin board behind my desk so that I could refer to them frequently in my planning. As the years passed, these gathered dust and eventually found their way into my long-term planning notebook. Later, they were relegated to a folder in my file cabinet.

When I began the intense collaboration of developing a new program, I wanted us to have a common curriculum model. Pat and I talked about curriculum values and directives. We reviewed traditional models. Eventually, I proposed a very simple model for our work. It is one we still use to determine the content of our teaching. We named it "Inside, Near, and Far." When we develop studies or assess our curriculum we ask questions relating to these three categories.

Inside is the work within the individual. In math, we are concerned with meaning and sense. We want our studies to help a child construct math scaffolding and patterns. These provide the basis for problem solving, decision making, and communication. In a study of geometry, we ask ourselves why a child would care. We wonder about a child's internal geometry. Does the child see the world in clearly defined figures? Can the child distinguish between an equilateral and isosceles triangle? We consider the child's enjoyment of math. We discuss a child's inquisitiveness.

The *near* component of math includes that which a child can experience directly. In geometry, *near* becomes the interaction with and manipulation of shapes. The child interacts with materials directly. We will use pattern blocks, building materials, or ice cubes. The child can feel the wood of patterns blocks. Touch develops correlative patterns in the brain. Anything the child can touch and see in and around the classroom enters the realm of *near*. Activities that require teamwork and collaboration are *near* activities. They are crucial to the child's construction of concepts.

The *far* side of curriculum is abstract. It is where ideas are considered and discussed and constructs of *near* are applied. *Far* in geometry considers the elliptical orbit of the planets, the gear ratio of clocks, discussions of energy efficient architecture, or the geometry of a painting. *Far* occurs when the child learns how the spherical globe is bisected by the equator.

These three strands of the curriculum intertwine and overlap. They help the children sort out their work. Disregarding them can lead to misunderstanding and miscommunication. When I attended a meeting of the planning commission of our city during which citizens were protesting a new development, the arguments never found common ground because participants were countering *near* concerns with *far* arguments. This behavior created tension and caused the meeting to extend into overtime. In the classroom, children learn to listen and respond to each other according to the origin of the speaker's point of view. When Eve says that a strategy doesn't make sense, she is talking about herself, not the strategy. She is describing a conflict within herself that occurs when the strategy does not match her constructs.

This is the *inside* for her. When she begins to work with a new idea using tens blocks or comparing strategies with another student, she is operating in the *near*. It is important to understand what is occurring inside of her. When she begins to synthesize ideas and develop rules to govern her strategies, she is synthesizing and applying. This is her *far* work. Knowing these strands, I can understand her questions and her work and communicate with her.

The Event-Specific Child

We were at a staff meeting, and the teachers were tired. The agenda was to address a problem of children's lack of respect for adults and school rules. The discussion began with statements of the problem. One teacher described a typical encounter.

"I stopped this child in the hall. I asked her to show me her pass to be in the building during lunch time. She responded with, 'I didn't know I needed one.' I reminded her that I had stopped her yesterday and told her about the rule. She said, 'I forgot.' I don't believe it. Selective memory is what I would call it."

The teacher was frustrated and I could understand why; however, this child happened to be in my class. She really did learn something in one event, then lacked the ability to retain and transfer it to a later event. I began noticing a trend in this type of behavior several years ago. Many of the children were affected by fetal alcohol or drugs. They pose a special concern to our curriculum and content. The girl in question at the meeting had struck me as very capable in math. In September, I had enjoyed working with her on strategies with fractions, but did find that she could not solve equations she had understood the previous day. She was more frustrated with herself than I was with her. We went back through the steps and she learned the work again. I found this pattern repeated time and again. Sometimes she would remember and sometimes she would forget. I had to model patience with her because anxiety was one of the surest precipitators of forgetfulness. My work with her was not training, because I was actually teaching her within each event. The work required willingness to repeat the process. I learned to streamline my teaching, reviewing the steps with only the pertinent information. Over time, strategies and skills became entrained within her. As her ability to retain her skills increased, so did her confidence and motivation. Her particular difficulty had resulted in a complicated confrontational behavior pattern that was not serving her. She had a reputation of defiance and incorrigibility. By developing math competency she began to form a base from which she could build self-confidence. She learned to accept her forgetfulness and diminish defensiveness around it. She developed the skill of articulating her condition and asking for help.

Art, Music, Math, and Physical Education

Over centuries and across cultures, people have known the importance of educating the mind and body. Aristotle advocated the teaching of gymnastics to build character before academics. Rudolph Steiner argued for the importance of developing artistic expression before academic study. From the Maori of New Zealand to the Innuit of the arctic regions, physical skills, songs and art preceded scholastics. In our culture, children worked and played at home. They climbed trees, jumped rope, and worked around the house and garden. They listened to music, created paper dolls, knitted, wove, baked, and participated in construction. Changes in the latter half of the twentieth century began to happen. Increasing urbanization overran forest and fields. The child of the city lost the climbing trees and playing fields. The introduction of television brought children inside. Packaged meals replaced the conversation and time management of cooking. Video games, home movies, and personal computers became common companions for children while parents worked away from home.

A public education that once had the luxury of ignoring physical development and focusing on academic had to re-examine its tasks. President Kennedy introduced the Presidential Fitness Standards. For a time, schools hired specialists and developed programs in physical education, art, and music. Programs flourished in the sixties and seventies. Then funding crises precipitated by tax limitations created scarcity. Programs and personnel were cut from budgets. These trends had ramifications for the teaching of mathematics.

I've Got Rhythm

Josh was a fifth grader who was intelligent, articulate, and had a great sense of humor. Yet math was a struggle for him. We had worked with him for five years and were unable to cultivate his mathematical sense. As we faced our last year with him, we were concerned. This year, Pam had joined our team. A musician specializing in guitar and drums, she was ready to create new learning with the children. As we sat around talking about Josh, I expressed my idea that I thought Josh lacked internal rhythm. He had no foundation to construct math patterns. Pam suggested that we try drumming. Pulling a group of students including Josh together, she began teaching drumming. It was difficult for Josh. Through Pam's observation of the group, we found a correlation between ease of learning the drum and math achievement. Josh struggled with drums. Eventually, he began to develop the ability to sustain beats and respond to rhythm. Our experiment lasted for only eight weeks, but it was enough to demonstrate limited success for Josh in math. His mental ability to learn patterns of multiplication facts and add numbers increased, and so did his self-confidence.

Our ability to negotiate the patterns and rhythms of math is strengthened through negotiating patterns and rhythms elsewhere. The brain learns the structure of pattern through physical activities such as walking, climbing, jumping, and running. A child develops patterns by collecting rocks, searching for a certain color, size, shape, or pattern on the ground. Holding a pattern in mind while looking for a match develops the same skills used in math. This is also true for playing catch with a ball, jumping rope while repeating rhymes, building with blocks, dribbling, or playing games. The physical sensation of rhythm is the foundation of development of pattern and rhythm in math. The decrease of these physical activities in our culture leads to complications in learning math. If I had a school with unlimited resources and funding, I would remove Josh from math class for three months and work with him to establish rhythm. I would have him drum and dance, map the times of days, months, and moon cycles, and develop ball skills. I would teach him to walk in rhythm.

I Discovered a Rhombus!

In post-graduate school, my daughter Katie worked with an art teacher who stressed the development of fundamental skills. She was painting a still life one day when she suddenly began to see the composition of this subject in geometric shapes. Though she had previous art analysis experience while drawing with shapes, there was something new in her way of seeing. She expressed it as an experience similar to staring at a three-dimensional poster and having it move into focus. Once seen, the experience can be re-created easily. In the ensuing weeks, doors opened for Katie. As she continued to incorporate geometry and proportion into her art, she began to look at her subjects differently. A mathematical harmony unveiled itself in her work. The correlation between the beauty of mathematics and the mathematics of art became an intrinsic part of her thought. Connections sparked in her mind. She saw math as a communication of adjectives; as with art, it was a set of comparisons. After her years of despising math, it was a sweet irony that her work with art was work in math. How can we allow each child to derive geometry and integrate it with their other concepts?

A friend of mine had a grandchild whose teacher attempted the same thing in fourth grade. After a study of geometry, she invited children to make a book representing the geometry of the world. Elliot loved fishing. He created a book called *The Geometric Fly Fishing Dictionary*. It showed the angles of a fish's mouth, a pentagonal figure of a tackle basket, and triangles of flies. He loved applying his passion to the study of geometry.

9
When Complexity Catches Up

Ian Malcolm was one of the most famous of the new generation of mathematicians who were openly interested in "how the real world works." These scholars broke with the cloistered tradition of mathematics in several important ways. For one thing, they used computers constantly, a practice traditional mathematicians frowned on. For another, they worked almost exclusively with nonlinear equations, in the emerging field called chaos theory. For a third, they appeared to care that their mathematics described something that actually existed in the real world.

—MICHAEL CRICHTON
Jurassic Park

In the book *Jurassic Park*, Malcolm describes a mathematical theory that foreshadows doom. Jurassic Park is an experiment to re-create dinosaurs in a controlled setting. Malcolm is describing Chaos Theory. He asserts that there are too many variables to control in this experiment to replicate the world of dinosaurs. Some of these variables will likely change the success of the venture into tragic failure. Failure is the outcome in this novel. The characters who do not heed Malcolm's warnings are intelligent, assumably college-educated professionals. They have taken math classes and understand variables.

Stories like Jurassic Park occur regularly in our society. Individuals, government agencies, and corporations act with disastrous ecological effects. There are too many variables to accurately predict. Instances abound in the biological world. As the agricultural revolution matured and demand for foods multiplied, farmers battled insect damage. Turning to biochemists for help, they were given DDT. It was a miracle agent that eliminated insects in their crops. It wasn't until twenty years later that some of the resultant variables became obvious. An alarming decline in birds of prey led to an investigation. Nest eggs were discovered that could not withstand the weight of the incubating parents. Further analysis demonstrated an accumulation of DDT in the parent birds that led to thin-shelled eggs. In a reversal of practice, DDT was banned in this country and millions of dollars were expended to revive the stricken bird populations.

Similar scenarios appear in the introduction of wild boar to Hawaii and consequent loss of native plant populations to these rooters. West coast salmon decline is linked to the forest practice of clearcutting near streams and rivers. The simple use of refrigerants and spray cans can contribute to the demise of our protective atmospheric ozone. When we try to solve equations rapidly and linearly, we simply cannot account for the complex variables and eventual ramifications.

The Sky Is Falling, The Sky Is Falling

There is certainly a time and a place for alarm, but as an elementary school teacher, I realize that alarm will only freeze children with fear and despair. We can, however, prepare children for crucial decision making by helping them to understand complexity and chaos. We can teach them to slow down and consider the relationship among the problem, solution, and the larger picture. In my school experience, I was frustrated to learn fields of study that were outdated or incomplete. It took more energy to clear my thinking of misconstructions and rebuild with authenticity than it would have to learn correct concepts in the first place. My conclusion was that my teachers had ceased to learn. They didn't maintain current reading and research and contented themselves with ignorance of new ideas in chemistry, math, and biology. It is our responsibility as teachers to maintain our learning and ideas and stay abreast of new work. As math teachers, we must learn Chaos Theory. Then we will be able to incorporate it into our math curriculum.

Butterflies in Brazil and Tornadoes in Texas

Edward Lorenz is credited with the discovery of Chaos Theory. He was working as a meteorologist. Attempting to solve the paradox of predicting the weather, Lorenz had an advantage over previous meteorologists. He had incorporated complex formulas into a computer program. Calculations could be rapidly analyzed. The year was 1962. He was computing equations with variables in the hundred-thousandths. Working late into the night, Lorenz decided to get a cup of coffee. Before leaving the computer, he initiated a program run but left off or truncated the last two decimal places. The variable ended at the thousandths place instead of the hundred-thousandths. It was a minor adjustment in the initial condition of the computation. Lorenz didn't expect any difference in the graphic solution printed by the computer. To his surprise, when he returned, the outcome was radically different. The graph was not at all similar to the previous ones. A very slight variation in the initial conditions, one ten-thousandth, had radically affected the outcome. Lorenz was astonished. Reflecting on a system as complex and global as weather, he realized it was affected by minute variables. He developed new ideas about meteorology. His famous explanation for the significant complexity of this theory was that a simple beat of a butterfly's wing in Brazil could set in motion a string of accumulating events that would result in a tornado in Texas. To Lorenz, the result appeared to be chaotic, so he named the theory Chaos. We can begin to grasp this theory by looking at some of its major components. Each of these has benefit to our work in the classroom.

Iteration

Teaching is cyclical. We have a beginning, a middle, and an end to our time with a group of students, then we begin again. As reflective teachers, each beginning is affected by the past cycles. Each starts at a slightly different place. Each cycle, be it a semester, a year, or longer is an iteration. Mathematically, an iteration names a single run through an equation containing multiple runs. Realizing that some of the variables are slightly altered by the equation, subsequent iterations will be different. In time, later iterations will appear significantly different from their initial counterparts, just like our teaching with years of experience will be different from our first year. There will, however, still remain commonalities. The teacher's personality, vocal tones, physical stature, and personal style add elements to the classroom that create recognizable patterns at each iteration.

Computers use iterations routinely as they are programmed with loops. They allow series of consecutive formulas to be executed. Asked to solve an equation such as $123(42 + x)$ when $x = 6$, the computer will create one hundred twenty-three binary movements. Asked to solve $123(42 + x)$ when $x = 6$, then feed the solution back into the equation as a new x, the computer will continue until stopped by an outside command.

Biologically iterations abound. The complex wildlife population systems grow and decline at fairly regular intervals. Trees grow annual rings. Salmon return to their river of birth after seven years at sea. Locusts emerge from the ground and dragonflies from the water. The same is true for physical science. The earth passes around the sun regularly giving us spring, summer, winter, and fall. Tides move between low and high, ebb and flow. It was by observing and calculating iterations that the people of Stonehenge were able to build an enormous structure over many decades to mark the sunrise at solstice. The ancients of Mexico designed cities that aligned with constellations on ceremonial occasions, some of which were on seventeen-year cycles.

Extending calculations through the use of iteration in the seventeenth century enabled Johannes Kepler to predict that huge sailing vessels would be able to rendezvous with Mars. It is the method present-day mathematicians use to calculate how a probe can leave earth at a variable speed and contact Jupiter at a precise location eleven years into the future.

Mathematicians recognize in all of these events that the iterations are not exact. Stonehenge no longer marks sunrise at solstice because of changes in the relationship between the sun and earth. Rendezvous with distant planets require slight adjustments that magnify with time. A child's style of constructing new learning will change with age.

Fractals

I am standing on a seashore watching the waves lap against the sand. The pattern they create makes me think of the breeze lapping the hills above me. The curved shape of the waves' upper reach is very much like the shape of these hills above. Changing scale I realize this pattern is the same as the ocean touching this entire coast. As my scale and perspective change, I see that each is a fractal of the other. The smaller systems metaphorically reflect the more complex.

After *Jurassic Park* introduced Chaos Theory to the general public, fractals captured our imagination. Fractal calendars and greeting cards entered the retail market. Posters and books of fractals appeared. Most of these are graphs of formulas produced by computer and enhanced by color. Visual representation of the poetry of math, they result from programming loop formulas into a computer for a given number of iterations. Loop formulas can be incorporated into class math problems.

> Mimi's uncle wanted some work done around his house. He offered to pay Mimi either a total of one hundred dollars or one penny for the first hour and double it each hour for a week. Which should Mimi accept?

Graphed, the solution to this problem would look like the fractals printed on calendars. I think of fractals as metaphors. To say that the falcon was a jet racing across the sky describes a visual comparison. Yet were we to create a graph and write a function for both falcon and jet, we would find that the speed, trajectory, and wind-resistant design are mathematically related. Similarly, a child in my class is a fractal of their parents and grandparents. Genetic encodement can determine closeness of iterations between siblings and parents. It can also show the relationship between humans and squirrels. Each iteration or generation leads to slight changes. Yet each is a fractal. By comparing genomes in a DNA molecule, we can determine the relative closeness of the fractal.

I have used fractals in the classroom directly. Showing a fractal graph, I have invited children to make their own fractals. They enjoy creating repeated patterns. It is similar to the work of creating a maze or mandala.

Mathematically, a simple fractal can be recorded on a t-chart. Pythagoras' triangular arrays offer a repeating design that can be graphed as follows.

Points	Triangles
3	1
6	5
10	12
15	21

```
                              x
                          x       x
                      x       x       x
                  x       x       x       x
              x       x       x       x       x
```

Fractals allow us to observe classroom practices and behavior indirectly. In Plato's shadow world, the actual principles are not directly observable. We infer them from the shadows. Similarly, we can see behaviors in our class that infer problems. When Eve begins to get frustrated, there are usually six or seven other students who are confused. When Jason is agitated, I can look for a stressor in the classroom environment that is affecting all of the children. Regarding spotted owls and anadromous salmon, the behavior of one species indicates the health of an ecosystem. Similarly, the behavior of one child indicates the current status of the classroom community.

This inferential process allowed Johannes Kepler in 1609 to chart the mountains on the moon by proportionately measuring their shadows. Currently it is used to study quantum particles of atoms. These particles cannot be observed directly, for the very process of observation alters them. They can be measured only by their effect on a very local environment.

The biological illustrator sees the ever-finer branching of a tree limb as a fractal similar to the branching of its roots. The same process occurs in the branching of our nervous system, lungs, and capillaries. Fractals bring us to similarities between systems. We begin to see a relationship between squirrel and birds, animal and environment, teacher and curriculum.

Initial Conditions

I sat in the staff room bemoaning my ineffectiveness with a child. The teacher I was talking to said, "You've got to consider the raw material with which you started." Each child comes to us with specific circumstances, attitude, and capacity. It is the reason we must match our instruction to the child. No class of mine has ever had the same capacity or passion as any other class. The initial conditions and our response to these conditions is what elevates our teaching to artistry.

In complex iterated formulas a slight variation in the initial conditions leads to radically different outcomes. Stephen Hawking has spent years investigating the beginnings of the universe. He concluded that a singular alteration at the beginning in something no larger than an electron, quantum, or neutrino would have altered the universe beyond anything we can imagine. Applied to ourselves, the implication leads to awe that we even exist. It spans the gap between science and miracle.

As teachers, we are instrumental in creating the initial conditions of our classroom. Each September, we envision what we want during the year for ourselves and the children we teach. We prepare the environment, materials, and curriculum to meet this vision. When the children come, they bring the main ingredient to the context. They too are the initial condition. Thus, we enter a relationship of presentation, determination, adjustment, and response. So diverse are these initial conditions that the outcome cannot be predicted with much precision. To effectively respond, we must be flexible in our vision of the outcome. Trying to achieve the same results with each child or group of children portends failure.

Phase Locking

Our class discussions often begin with an undifferentiated direction. Children are building on each other and momentum directs the discussion. During initial dialogue, ideas are expressed and many observations made. When Eve was in class, she would grasp one of these statements and make exception or want to pursue it. The class would become agitated and frustrated, wanting to continue with an evolving discussion. It was as if there were an unspoken consensus on where the discussion was leading, and she was resisting the direction. Eve obviously was not part of the consensus. In their frustration, tempers would develop and criticisms emerge. After noting and reflecting on this pattern a few times, I decided to try to explain a part of Chaos Theory to the children. I introduced the idea of complex systems by describing a river. The water in the river is a complex system, moving through a sculpted landscape. It has momentum, and it is predictable. Like a discussion, it is a system in phase. When an unusual event such as extra rainfall or sudden snow melt enters this system it can create change. In this case, the river may flood. The system becomes chaotic, unpredictable. The change can be temporary until the water recedes and the banks reclaim the river. Sometimes, the system change can come in the form of a dam. External forces enter and control the river. A completed dam institutes a new phase in the water's flow. Now the system includes a reservoir. Our discussion was like a river beginning to form a phase. A direction would start to become apparent to class members. Then Eve interrupted the discussion and it became locked in a single spot, like the dam of the river. In response, the children felt stopped, cut off from the direction they had intended. It locked the momentum into a new phase. This gave Eve a visual image. She understood the concept and began to see the relationship between her phase locking and the frustration of the class. It gave all of us vocabulary to articulate the process.

Teachers become phase locked when they pull out lesson plans written in years past. They expect to teach a new group, with new initial conditions, the same way they taught a previous group. Such a condition does not maximize learning. If the curriculum is phase locked, response and partnership cannot occur. Construction is stifled. Someone must adjust. Sometimes phase locking can be helpful. As teachers, we like to enter a phase of familiarity in the geography of our work. We teach one age group for one or more school years. The opposite would mean constantly moving classrooms and changing age levels of children. Such a situation would produce stress and chaos. As teachers, we look for a system that has the dynamics of chaos and the stability of comfort without stagnation. We adjust some things to a specific class while keeping other components regular.

Bifurcation

Each year, the moon moves a fraction of a millimeter away from earth. Though it is phase locked in its orbit by the gravitational pull of earth, its thrust causes a slight variation with each iteration. Eventually, the moon will move far enough away so that the momentum of thrust will overcome the momentum of gravity and the orbital system will enter chaos. The moon will swing around earth and shoot off into space. Mathematically predicted to occur in a couple of million years, that moment will be the bifurcation point. The bifurcation point is the instance when the system changes. A saturated hill turns into a landslide. A frustrated child bursts into tears. An inquisitive person grasps a new concepts. All of these are moments of bifurcation. Sometimes the moment carries the system into bifurcation with predictable outcomes. Sometimes the bifurcation is a surprise and sometimes it is a choice. When we encounter behaviors in a child that frustrate us, we have a moment to choose whether to be patient or abrupt, whether to listen or talk. It is a crucial moment in this particular relationship and our considerate choice can determine the outcome. Patience may produce new understanding and greater trust. Abruptness may inhibit inquiry and understanding.

Mathematically, size and complexity are usually the determinants of bifurcation. When a system becomes cumbersome it bifurcates. Equations that add more and more variables will eventually move to a new generation of solutions. Bees that overpopulate a hive will divide into two groups. A heart that is overloaded with cholesterol-filled arteries will fail. One extra straw will break the camel's back.

Complexity gives me a lens to view the world in which all the variables interrelate. Seemingly unrelated and insignificant events have meaning I didn't predict. It invites me to honor parts of our classroom that we may have previously overlooked. I begin to see the interrelatedness of complex components in our learning community.

10

So What?

It is a most extraordinary thing that although most of us are opposed to political tyranny and dictatorship, we inwardly accept the authority, the tyranny, of another to twist our minds and our way of life.
— J. KRISHNAMURTI

In 1998, El Niño struck the West coast of the United States with storms bringing record rainfall and enormous waves. In the face of waves, city, county, and state crews brought bulldozers onto the beach and built sand walls to protect shoreline homes. It was a valiant but futile effort. Anyone who spent time on the beach as a child knew that moats and walls around sand castles only delayed the inevitable destruction by the sea. We can only occupy the sand for a short time, never own it and preserve it.

When Learning Belongs to Children

Children know how to ask the questions "why?", "so?", or "so what?" but they don't often get a chance to explore them. "So what?" asks what difference does this math make? What other uses will it have for me now or in the future? For years, I was the gate keeper of learning in my classroom. I informed students of the importance of their work. I explained why they would need these skills in life. Sometimes my rationale was that they would need these skills in high school. Sometimes I explained the application of math to adult life. Always, I felt put off by the questions. It was not until I developed my constructivist practices and began reflecting on my teaching that I became sensitive enough to realize they didn't care about my "so what's." If my reasons for learning were believed, they were not self-motivating. I was surprised at first. In jest, I answered "so what?" questions with nonsense. Sometimes they realized I had switched to nonsense, sometimes they didn't. Finally, one day after they had caught my nonsensical "so what," I asked them why they thought a particular lesson was important. I wasn't looking for a child-generated rendition of what I would answer, but genuinely wanted to know what they thought. We had been investigating perimeter. Sam thought that it would help her work with her mother as they designed a playhouse for her. Jamie thought he might use it to build a fence for his dog. Children began to brainstorm the possible uses of perimeters. I could see the math lesson begin to extend into the culture of their lives. They generated reasons for their work. "So what" became a habit for the class. They looked forward to sharing their ideas after math workshop. In anticipation they began to imagine use for their work throughout the workshop. More and more students caught on and soon we had added this new element to our culture. It is an important part of our response to learning events. It bridges experiences in school with their activities outside of school. We explore the "so what" through class discussions. Sometimes it takes individual conferences with children before they can understand the task of writing their "so what." When they start responding, "so what" log entries are often generic: "Next time I'll be able to solve this kind of problem more quickly." The content of these early responses is not as important as taking the time to ask the question and consider answers. At the end of math workshop, I ask children to respond in the logs. Responses include a description of what they did during the workshop, what they were thinking about, feelings, and "so what." Children examine their work and determine its significance. Sometimes they see obvious connections. Other times they don't. Either way, it is important for them to analyze the significance of the work they undertake.

Our role as educators is changing. Information explodes beyond our capacity to teach it. For a while, schools attempted to add content to curriculum to keep up with the social and cultural information explosion. When computers first appeared, educators taught basic language and programming skills. Binary systems were part of our curriculum. The evolution of computer technology soon outdistanced our capacity to provide understandable curriculum in elementary school. We find ourselves in a similar situation in science. In 1998, sheep and cows were cloned. A probe landed on Mars and explored the surface by remote, analyzing mineralogy through x-rays. Scientists were planning methods to strip mine ice on the moon in order to create a space rocket-fuel station. Smart missiles could annihilate a single building in a metropolitan area from a thousand miles away. Astrophysicists chased the edge of the universe while atomic physicists studied subparticles that blink in and out of matter. In the face of this, what difference does our day's activity make?

In response, public education enters a bifurcation point. It is a system that has been phase locked for a century. Changes have been no more than the occasional widening of a river bend or deepening of a channel. They are slight variations. As our culture explodes with information that will shatter our world view, education hesitates to embrace change. It sits at a crossroad. Will it continue in its present course until it is obsolete? If so, it will divorce from the direction of cultural knowledge. We will direct our teaching to what was and create a schism between groups of people who will continue to learn current research, problems, and decisions and those who won't know. Or public education can foresee the outcome of the knowledge explosion. Realizing that we can no longer teach the accumulation of content, we will begin to teach children. We will guide them to develop strategies to learn and respond to knowledge that we do not presently imagine. We will partner with them for the future.